TREES AND SHRUBS FOR TEMPERATE CLIMATES

TREES AND SHRUBS FOR TEMPERATE CLIMATES

Third Revised Edition

GORDON COURTRIGHT

TIMBER PRESS
Portland, Oregon

1st printing 1979
2nd edition 1984
3rd edition 1988

ISBN 0-88192-097-5

Printed in Hong Kong

Timber Press
9999 SW Wilshire
Portland, Oregon 97225

LIBRARY OF CONGRESS
Library of Congress Cataloging-in-Publication Data

Courtright, Gordon.
    Trees and shrubs for temperate climates / Gordon Courtright. --
3rd rev. ed.
        p.   cm.
    Rev. ed. of: Trees and shrubs for western gardens. c1979.
    Includes indexes.
    ISBN 0-88192-097-5 : $43.00
    1. Ornamental woody plants--Identification. 2. Ornamental woody
plants--Pictorial works.   I. Courtright, Gordon. Trees and shrubs
for western gardens. II. Title.
SB435.C793 1988
    635.9'77--dc19   87-36433
                                                           CIP

CONTENTS

This book is intended to be a visual plant dictionary.

DEDICATION

This book is dedicated to my good wife, Addi, without whose unending help and continual encouragement this work would never have been completed.

ACKNOWLEDGMENTS

I wish to express my thanks to the many, many people who helped me along the way. Some for sharing their knowledge about certain plants, some for directing me to good specimens suitable for photography. Special thanks to the following who helped so much when I most needed help.

Mrs. Mai K. Arbegast, Landscape Architect, Berkeley, California.

Dr. Howard C. Brown, Dean of Agriculture and Natural Resources, California Polytechnic College, San Luis Obispo, California.

Mr. John Bryan, Horticultural Consultant, Sausalito, California.

Professor E. Wesley Conner, Department of Horticulture, California Polytechnic College, San Luis Obispo, California.

Mr. Tom Courtright, my son, Nurseryman, Lafayette, California.

Mr. Glen Handy, Nurseryman, Portland, Oregon.

Mr. Julian Herman, Photographer, North Hollywood, California.

Mr. J. Ken Lister, Nurseryman, Gladstone, Oregon.

Mrs. Celia Wittenber, Consultant, Sausalito, California.

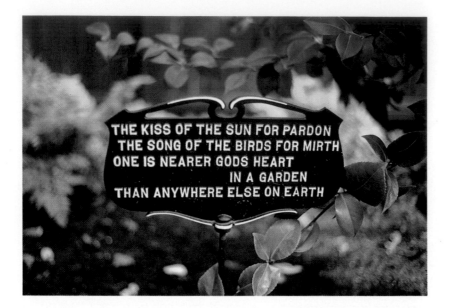

INTRODUCTION

This book is intended to be a practical visual dictionary of all the plants readily obtainable in temperate climate retail nurseries. It is not intended to replace the many excellent botanies written to encompass the many plants sometimes used in gardening. My motive in writing this book grew out of the practical gardening problems I encountered in 40 years of the nursery business trying to assist homeowners with their plant requirements.

The numerous books written from a botanic point of view have sent gardeners to nurseries looking for plants not commonly propagated and sold. This experience, repeated thousands of times yearly, only leads to frustration for both the misguided and ultimately disappointed gardener and the nurseryman with hundreds of plants in stock, which will serve the gardener's intended purpose equally well. So the first guiding principle of this book is to lead gardeners to the hundreds of fine plants commonly available in the trade which have proved themselves as especially suitable for the growing conditions of the Temperate Zone throughout the world.

Second, unlike other gardening books that usually are organized by plant families, I have divided the plants into sections by typical height and type, i.e., Low-Growing Shrubs, Medium-Growing Shrubs, Tall-Growing Shrubs, Trees, Vines, and Conifers. I recognize that the height categories will not be entirely valid in all areas throughout the world—first, because plants grow differently in one climatic area than another and, further, because many plants are sold (on landscape plans, etc.) to be kept pruned to a given height where they look best.

I have organized the plants by these growth characteristics as a result of my nursery experience. Over the years, I found that most customers came to the nursery looking for a plant to fulfill a specific purpose in a specific place. Frequently, their choice of a specific plant was made from a description in a general horticultural book wherein height and width are seldom mentioned. Hence, the second guiding principle of this book is that of growth characteristics so that the reader will not be disappointed by choosing a plant quite unsuitable for its place or purpose.

This principle has been adhered to throughout the book—with the exception of *Azaleas* (all of which will be found in Low-Growing Shrubs) and *Rhododendrons* (all of which will be found in Medium-Growing Shrubs) and of the Ferns, all listed in the medium section, and the Palms, which are in the tall section. So, if your planting plans call for a low plant, all the low-growing shrubs are to be found in one section in a group together, each accompanied by a color picture.

Third, I have used the language of a nursery catalog, not a botanic book. All too frequently I have found that the scientific nomenclature of the botanist has escaped the lay reader interested only in the beauty of the garden. The language I have chosen I hope will assist the reader's comprehension of the plant available material.

The plants in each section are listed alphabetically by their botanic names with the common names added. I have followed the names used by the leading, large wholesale nurseries in the United States. I have included the newer names being introduced by the nomenclature committee on plant names. If you know only the common name of a plant look in the List of Common to Botanic Names on pages 225 to 231 to guide you to the plant you are seeking.

I have provided two numeric planting indexes for each plant. The first is a temperature guide, shown as temperature zone below which a plant cannot withstand the cold. The second is a planting guide number which indicates the broad cultural requirements of the plant—exposure to sun, drainage, and soil requirements.

Thus Zone 9 means the plant's freezing resistance is somewhere between 30° and 20° Fahrenheit, depending on how well the plant has hardened off in the fall. But, remember, that many will freeze at 27° or 28°, so the zone guide is merely a clue to put you on your guard.

The same care must be exercised in using the planting guide number. A specific plant may depart slightly in its cultural requirements from those indicated—so use common sense in planting it in a specific location.

Detailed explanations of the meaning of the Zone and Planting Guides will be found immediately following this Introduction and in other places in the book.

In choosing the specimens to illustrate each plant it has been my aim to pick subjects in the five to fifteen year old size. I have endeavored to locate plants that stand alone when possible. In some cases, however, particularly in the case of large, bushy plants, vines, and hedge plants, I have used a closeup to portray only the foliage in about a one square foot area.

I chose to photograph plants in garden settings rather than using nursery plants in a studio setting, not only to give the reader an accurate impression of what might be expected of the plants in the garden, but also to present landscaping ideas that might prove useful.

The selection of plants included is based entirely on the catalogues of a number of the largest wholesale nurseries. Some plants listed in these catalogues were excluded because they are closely related to or indistinguishable variations of plants.

Following the plant listings you will find a number of indexes to provide you with specific information or particular characteristics. Included are:

Planting guide.

Temperature guide.

Botanic name to common name with plate number and
   pronunciation dictionary.

Common name to botanic name.

White flowering plants.

Yellow and orange flowering plants.

Blue and violet flowering plants.

Red or pink flowering plants.

Plants suitable for seashore.

Fragrant trees and shrubs.

Plants for dry places.

Plants for damp places.

A deer-resistant plant list.

An oak root fungus list.

It is my sincere hope that you, the reader, find this work a useful and practical guide to the solution of your gardening problems. If you do, I will feel completely rewarded for the full-time job I have had since I retired from the nursery business.

ZONE AND PLANTING GUIDES

Following each description is a planting group guide. Here, again, individual conditions will vary, so the planting instructions are general. An attempt has been made to give you a clue to the general soil conditions needed for each plant. You should check local conditions with your nursery.

Group 1 means the plant will grow in the sun without special treatment, unless otherwise mentioned.

Group 2 means the plant will grow in the sun, but must have excellent drainage.

Group 3 means the plant will grow in the sun, but must have excellent drainage and only minimum amounts of water, usually gray foliage plants.

Group 4 means the plant will grow in the shade, without special treatment.

Group 5 means the plant will grow in the shade, but must have excellent drainage and special soil mixture.

TEMPERATURE RATINGS

Zone 10	40° to 30° F
Zone 9	30° to 20° F
Zone 8	20° to 10° F
Zone 7	10° to 0° F
Zone 6	0° to −10° F
Zone 5	−10° to −20° F
Zone 4	−20° to −30° F
Zone 3	−30° to −40° F

Temperatures suggested in this book are approximate. The growing conditions, for example, a warm, late fall, often will keep the plants from hardening off and a sudden, early, cold snap has been known to freeze plants 20° above the normal freezing point.

BOTANIC INDEX

BOTANIC NAME	PRONUNCIATION	COMMON NAME	PLATE NUMBER
Abelia 'Edward Goucher'	A-beel-i-a	Pink Abelia	111
Abelia grandiflora		Glossy Abelia	112
Abies balsamea 'Nana'	Ay-bees	Dwarf Balsam Fir	569
Abies concolor		White Fir	570
Abies lasiocarpa		Alpine Fir	571
Abies pinsapo 'Glauca'		Blue Spanish Fir	572
Abutilon hybridum	A-beau-ti-lon	Flowering Maple	113
Acacia baileyana	A-kay-shi-a	Bailey or Fernleaf Acacia	369
Acacia baileyana 'Purpurea'		Purple Leaf Acacia	370
Acacia longifolia		Sydney Golden Wattle	371
Acacia melanoxylon		Blackwood Acacia	372
Acacia verticillata		Star Acacia	373
Acanthus mollis	A-kanth-us	Bear's Breech	1
Acer circinatum	Ay-ser	Vine Maple	374
Acer japonicum 'Aconitifolium'		Fern-leaf Full-moon Maple	375
Acer palmatum		Japanese Maple	376
Acer palmatum 'Atropurpureum'		Red Japanese Maple	377
Acer palmatum 'Dissectum'		Red Cutleaf Maple	2
Acer palmatum 'Dissectum Ever Red'		Red Cutleaf Maple	3
Acer palmatum 'Dissectum Viridis'		Japanese Green Cutleaf Maple	4
Acer palmatum 'Sangokaku'		Japanese Coral Bark Maple	378
Acer platanoides		Norway Maple	379
Acer platanoides 'Crimson King'		Crimson King Maple	381
Acer platanoides 'Schwedleri'		Schwedler Purple Leaf Maple	380
Acer saccharinum		Silver Maple	382
Adiantum pedatum	Ad-i-an-tum	Five Finger Fern	167
Aesculus carnea 'Briotii'	Es-keu-lus	Red Horse Chestnut	383

BOTANIC NAME	PRONUNCIATION	COMMON NAME	PLATE NUMBER
Aesculus hippocastanum		White Horse Chestnut	384
Agapanthus africanus	Ag-a-pan-thus	Lily of the Nile	5
Agapanthus africanus 'Peter Pan'		Dwarf Lily of the Nile	6
Agave attenuata	Ah-gah-ve	Agave	7
Albizia julibrissin	Al-biz-i-a	Silktree; Pink Acacia; Mimosa	385
Alnus cordata	All-nus	Italian Alder	386
Alnus rhombifolia		White Alder	387
Aloysia triphylla see *Lippia citriodora*			
Alsophila australis	Al-sof-il-a	Australian Tree Fern	168
Althaea syriaca	Althee-a	Rose of Sharon	114
Ampelopsis quinquefolia	Am-pe-lop-sis	Virginia Creeper	522
Ampelopsis tricuspidata		Boston Ivy	523
Andromeda polifolia	An-drom-e-da	Bog Rosemary	8
Aralia elegantissima	A-ray-lia	False Aralia	115
Aralia papyrifera		Rice Paper Plant	261
Aralia sieboldii		Glossy Aralia	116
Araucaria araucana	Ahr-a-kair-ia	Monkey Tree	573
Araucaria bidwillii		Bunya-Bunya	574
Araucaria excelsa		Star or Norfolk Island Pine	575
Araucaria heterophylla see *A. excelsa*			
Arbutus menziesii	Ar-bu-tus	Madrone	388
Arbutus unedo		Strawberry Tree	262
Arbutus unedo 'Compacta'		Dwarf Strawberry Tree	117
Archontophoenix cunninghamiana see *Seaforthia elegans*			
Arctostaphylos densiflora 'Howard McMinn'	Ark-to-staf-il-os	Howard McMinn Manzanita	9
Arctostaphylos hookeri		Monterey Manzanita	10
Arctostaphylos uva ursi		Kinnikinnick or Bear Berry	11
Arecastrum romanzoffianum see *Cocos plumosa*			
Asparagus densiflorus 'Meyers'	As-par-a-gus	Meyeri	169
Asparagus densiflorus 'Sprengeri'		Sprengeri	170
Aspidistra elatior	As-pi-dis-tra	Cast Iron Plant	12
Aspidium capense	As-pid-i-um	Leather Leaf Fern	171
Asplenium bulbiferum	As-plee-ni-um	Mother Fern	172
Aucuba japonica	Au-keu-ba	Dwarf Aucuba	118
Aucuba japonica 'Crotonifolia'		Croton Leaf Aucuba	119
Aucuba japonica 'Picturata'		Gold Leaf Aucuba	120
Aucuba japonica 'Variegata'		Gold Dust Plant	121
Azaleas	A-zay-le-a	Azalea *(Rhododendron)*	13–13X
Azara microphylla	A-za-ra	Box Leaf Azara	263
Bambusa phyllostachys 'Aurea'	Bam-bu-sa	Golden Bamboo	264
Bambusa phyllostachys 'Bambusoides'		Giant Timber Bamboo	265
Bambusa phyllostachys 'Nigra'		Black Bamboo	266
Bambusa sasa 'Pygmaea'		Dwarf Bamboo	14
Bauhinia purpurea	Ba-hin-i-a	Orchid Tree	389
Beaucarnea recurvata	Bo-car-ne-a	Bottle Ponytail	267

BOTANIC NAME	PRONUNCIATION	COMMON NAME	PLATE NUMBER
Beaumontia grandiflora	Bo-mon-ti-a	Easter Lily Vine	524
Beloperone guttata	Bel-o-per-o-ne	Shrimp Plant	15
Berberis darwinii	Ber-ber-is	Darwin Barberry	122
Berberis julianae		Wintergreen Barberry	123
Berberis thunbergii 'Atropurpurea'		Red Leaf Japanese Barberry	124
Bergenia cordifolia see *Saxifraga rubicunda*			
Betula alba	Bet-u-la	European White Birch	390
Betula alba laciniata		Cutleaf Weeping Birch	391
Betula alba 'Youngii'		Young's Weeping Birch	392
Betula papyrifera		Canoe or Paper Birch	393
Betula pendula see *B. alba*			
Bignonia cherere	Big-non-ia	Scarlet Trumpet Vine	525
Bignonia venusta		Flame Vine	526
Bignonia violacea		Lavender Trumpet Vine	527
Bougainvillea (In Variety)	Bou-gayn-vil-le-a	Bougainvillea	528–534
Bouvardia 'Albatross'	Bo-var-di-a	White Bouvardia	16
Bouvardia longiflora see *B.* 'Albatross'			
Brachychiton populneus see *Sterculia diversifolia*			
Brahea armata see *Erythea armata*			
Brahea edulis see *Erythea edulis*			
Brugmansia suaveolens see *Datura suaveolens*			
Brunfelsia calycina floribunda	Brun-fel-si-a	Yesterday, Today and Tomorrow Shrub	125
Brunfelsia pauciflora 'Floribunda' see *B. calycina* 'Floribunda'*			
Butia capitata see *Cocos australis*			
Buxus japonica	Buk-sus	Japanese Boxwood	17
Buxus microphylla japonica see *B. japonica*			
Buxus sempervirens		English Boxwood	126
Buxus sempervirens 'Suffruticosa'		Dwarf English Boxwood	18
Caesalpinia gilliesii see *Poinciana gilliesii*			
Calliandra haematocephala see *C. inequilatera*			
Calliandra inequilatera	Kal-i-an-dra	Pink Powder Puff	127
Calliandra tweedii		Brazilian Flame Bush	128
Callistemon citrinus see *C. lanceolatus*			
Callistemon lanceolatus	Kal-li-ste-mon	Red or Lemon Bottlebrush	268/394
Callistemon viminalis		Weeping Bottlebrush	269/395
Calluna vulgaris 'H. E. Beale'	Ka-lu-na	Pink Scotch Heather	19
Calluna vulgaris 'Searlei'		Scotch Heather	20
Calocedrus decurrens see *Libocedrus decurrens*			
Camellias	Ka-mel-i-a		129–130
Camphora officinarum	Kamp-for	Camphor Tree	396
Campsis tagliabuana 'Madame Galen'	Kamp-sis	Trumpet Creeper	535
Carissa grandiflora	Ka-ris-a	Natal Plum	131
Carissa grandiflora 'Tuttle'		Dwarf Natal Plum	21
Carissa macrocarpa see *C. grandiflora*			

BOTANIC NAME	PRONUNCIATION	COMMON NAME	PLATE NUMBER
Carissa macrocarpa 'Tuttle' see *Carissa grandiflora* 'Tuttle'			
Carpenteria californica	Kar-pen-te-ri-a	Bush Anemone	270
Carpinus betulus 'Columnaris'	Kar-pin-us	European Hornbeam	397
Cassia artemisioides	Kas-si-a	Wormwood Senna	132
Catalpa speciosa	Ka-tal-pa	Western Catalpa	398
Ceanothus arboreus 'Ray Hartman'	See-a-no-thus	Ray Hartman Ceanothus	271
Ceanothus cyaneus 'Sierra Blue'		Sierra Blue Ceanothus	272
Ceanothus gloriosus		Point Reyes Creeper	22
Ceanothus griseus horizontalis		Carmel Creeper	23
Ceanothus impressus		Santa Barbara Ceanothus	133
Ceanothus 'Julia Phelps'			134
Ceanothus 'Mountain Haze'			135
Cedrus atlantica	Se-drus	Atlas Cedar	576
Cedrus atlantica 'Glauca'		Blue Atlas Cedar	577
Cedrus atlantica 'Glauca Pendula'		Weeping Blue Atlas Cedar	578
Cedrus deodara		California Christmas Tree	579
Cedrus deodara 'Aurea'		Golden Deodar	580
Cedrus deodara 'Prostrata'		Weeping Deodar	581
Cedrus libani		Cedar of Lebanon	582
Ceratonia siliqua	Ser-a-tone-i-a	Carob or St. John's Bread	399
Ceratostigma plumbaginoides	Ser-a-to-stig-ma	Blue Leadwort	24
Cercis canadensis	Ser-sis	Eastern Redbud	273
Cercis occidentalis		Western Redbud	274
Cestrum parqui	Ses-trum	Night Blooming Jessamine	136
Chaenomeles japonica see *Cydonia japonica*			
Chamaecyparis lawsoniana	Kam-e-sip-a-ris	Port Orford Cedar; Lawson Cypress	583
Chamaecyparis lawsoniana 'Allumii'		Blue Lawson Cypress	584
Chamaecyparis lawsoniana 'Ellwoodii'		Ellwood Cypress	585
Chamaecyparis lawsoniana 'Nidiformis'		Birdnest Cypress	586
Chamaecyparis obtusa		Hinoki Cypress	587
Chamaecyparis obtusa 'Aurea'		Golden Hinoki Cypress	588
Chamaecyparis obtusa 'Crippsii'		Cripps Golden Cypress	589
Chamaecyparis obtusa 'Minima'			590
Chamaecyparis obtusa 'Nana'		Dwarf Hinoki Cypress	591
Chamaecyparis obtusa 'Torulosa'		Twisted Hinoki Cypress	592
Chamaecyparis pisifera 'Cyano Viridis'		Blue Plume Cypress	593
Chamaecyparis pisifera 'Filifera'		Threadbranch Cypress	594
Chamaecyparis pisifera 'Filifera Aurea'		Golden Threadbranch Cypress	594
Chamaecyparis pisifera 'Plumosa'		Plume Cypress	595
Chamaerops excelsa	Ka-me-rops	Windmill Palm	317
Chamaerops humilis		Mediterranean Fan Palm	318
Chamelaucium ciliatum	Kam-ae-lau-si-um	Geraldton Wax Flower	137
Chamelaucium uncinatum see *C. ciliatum*			
Choisya ternata	Choice-c-a	Mexican Orange	138

BOTANIC NAME	PRONUNCIATION	COMMON NAME	PLATE NUMBER
Chorisia speciosa	Ko-ris-e-a	Floss Silk Tree	400
Cinnamomum camphora see *Camphora officinarum*			
Cissus antarctica	Sis-us	Kangaroo Ivy	536
Cissus capensis		Evergreen Grape	537
Cissus rhombifolia		Grape Ivy	538
Cistus corbariensis	Sis-tus	White Rock Rose	25
Cistus hybridus see *C. corbariensis*			
Cistus ladanifera maculatus		Crimson Spot Rock Rose	26
Cistus purpureus		Orchid Spot Rock Rose	27
Citrus	Sit-rus		139–142
Clematis (Deciduous; In Variety)	Klem-a-tis	Clematis	540–540K
Clematis armandii		Evergreen Clematis	539
Clivia miniata	Kli-vi-a	Kafir Lily	28
Clytostoma callistegioides see *Bignonia violacea*			
Cocculus laurifolius	Kok-u-lus	Laurelleaf Snail Seed	275
Cocos australis	Ko-kus	Hardy Blue Cocos	319
Cocos plumosa		Queen Palm	320
Coleonema album see *Diosma ericoides*			
Coleonema pulchrum see *Diosma pulchrum*			
Convolvulus cneorum	Kon-vol-veu-lus	Bush Morning Glory	29
Coprosma baueri	Ko-pros-ma	Mirror Plant	143
Coprosma baueri 'Aurea'		Golden Mirror Plant	30
Coprosma kirkii		Creeping Mirror Plant	31
Coprosma repens see *C. baurei*			
Cordyline indivisa see *Dracaena indivisa*			
Cordyline stricta	Kor-di-li-ne	Palm Lily	144
Cornus florida	Kor-nus	White Flowering Dogwood	401
Cornus florida 'Rubra'		Pink Flowering Dogwood	402
Cornus florida 'Welchii'		Tricolor Dogwood	403
Cornus nuttallii		Western Dogwood	404
Cornus nuttallii 'Goldspot'		Goldspot Dogwood	405
Corokia cotoneaster	Cor-ok-e-a	Cotoneaster Corokia	145
Correa pulchella	Kor-re-a	Australian Fuchsia	32
Cortaderia selloana	Kor-ta-der-i-a	Pampas Grass	276
Corylus avellana 'Contorta'	Kor-i-lus	Twisted Filbert; Walking Stick	146
Cotinus coggygria	Ko-ti-nus	Smoke Tree	277
Cotoneaster dammeri	Ko-to-ne-as-ter	Bearberry Cotoneaster	33
Cotoneaster franchetii		Franchet Cotoneaster	279
Cotoneaster glaucophyllus		Bright Bead Cotoneaster	34
Cotoneaster horizontalis		Rock Cotoneaster	35
Cotoneaster lacteus 'Parneyi' see *C. parneyi*			
Cotoneaster microphyllus		Rockspray Cotoneaster	36
Cotoneaster pannosus		Silverleaf Cotoneaster	280
Cotoneaster parneyi		Red Clusterberry Cotoneaster	281
Crassula argentea	Kras-u-la	Jade Plant	147

BOTANIC NAME	PRONUNCIATION	COMMON NAME	PLATE NUMBER
Crassula ovata see *C. argentea*			
Crataegus contorta	Kra-te-gus	Snake Hawthorn	148
Crataegus cordata		Washington Thorn	406
Crataegus laevigata 'Coccinea Flore Pleno' see *C. oxyacantha* 'Paulii'			
Crataegus lavallei		Carrierei Hawthorn	407
Crataegus oxyacantha 'Paulii'		Paul's Scarlet Hawthorn	408
Crataegus phaenopyrum see *C. cordata*			
Crotalaria agatiflora	Krot-a-la-ri-a	Canary Bird Bush	149
Cryptomeria japonica 'Elegans'	Krip-to-me-ri-a	Plume Cedar	596
Cryptomeria japonica 'Elegans Nana'		Compact Plume Cedar	597
Cupaniopsis anacardioides	Cup-ain-e-op-is	Carrotwood	409
Cupressocyparis leylandii	Kew-press-o-sip-a-ris	Leyland Cypress	598
Cupressus glabra see *Cupressus arizonica*			
Cupressus macrocarpa	Ku-press-us	Monterey Cypress	600
Cupressus sempervirens 'Glauca'		Italian Cypress	601
Cycas revoluta	Sy-kas	Sago Palm	321
Cydonia japonica	Sy-doh-ni-a	Flowering Quince	150
Cyperus alternifolius	Sy-per-os	Umbrella Flatsedge	37
Cyperus papyrus		Egyptian Paper Reed	282
Cyrtomium falcatum	Ser-to-mi-um	Holly Fern	173
Cytisus (In Variety)	Si-tis-us	Scotch Broom	151–155
Cytisus racemosus see *Genista racemosa*			
Daphne burkwoodii 'Somerset'	Daf-ne		38
Daphne cneorum		Garland Daphne	39
Daphne odora		Winter Daphne	40
Datura suaveolens	Day-tu-ra	Angel's Trumpet	283
Daubentonia tripetii	Daub-en-ton-ia	Scarlet Wisteria Tree	156
Deutzia gracilis	Dut-zi-a	Deutzia	41
Dicksonia antarctica	Dick-so-ne-a	Tasmanian Tree Fern	174
Dietes iridioides see *Moraea iridioides*			
Diosma ericoides	Di-oz-ma	Baby's Breath; Breath of Heaven	42
Diosma pulchrum		Pink Breath of Heaven	43
Diospyros kaki	Dy-os-po-ros	Persimmon	410
Distictis buccinatoria see *Bignonia cherere*			
Dizygotheca elegantissima see *Aralia elegantissima*			
Dodonaea viscosa 'Purpurea'	Do-don-ea	Purple Leafed Hopseed Bush	284/411
Dracaena indivisa	Dra-se-na	Blue Draecena	285
Echium fastuosum	Ek-i-um	Pride of Madeira	157
Eleagnus pungens	El-ee-agnus	Silver Berry	286
Eleagnus pungens 'Maculata'		Gold Edge Eleagnus	287
Ensete ventricosum see *Musa ensete*			
Ensete ventricosum 'Maurelii' see *Musa maurelii*			
Equisetum hyemale	Ek-wi-se-tum	Horsetail Reed Grass	44

BOTANIC NAME	PRONUNCIATION	COMMON NAME	PLATE NUMBER
Erica canaliculata see *E. melanthera*			
Erica carnea 'Springwood'	E-ri-ka	Spring Heath	45/46
Erica melanthera 'Rosea'		Pink Scotch Heather	158
Eriobotrya deflexa	E-ri-bot-ri-a	Bronze Loquat	412
Eriobotrya japonica		Loquat	413
Eriogonum arborescens	Er-i-ogon-um	Santa Cruz Island Buckwheat	47
Erythea armata	Er-i-the-a	Mexican Blue Palm	322
Erythea edulis		Guadalupe Palm	323
Escallonia bifida see *E. montevidensis*			
Escallonia exoniensis 'Fradesii' see *E.* 'Fradesii'			
Escallonia 'Fradesii'	Es-ka-lon-ia	Pink Princess Escallonia	288
Escallonia laevis see *E. organensis*			
Escallonia montevidensis		White Escallonia	289
Escallonia organensis		Pink Escallonia	290
Escallonia rubra		Red Escallonia	160
Eucalyptus citriodora	U-ka-lip-tus	Lemon Scented Gum	414
Eucalyptus ficifolia		Red Flowering Gum	415/416
Eucalyptus globulus		Blue Gum	417
Eucalyptus globulus 'Compacta'		Dwarf Blue Gum	418
Eucalyptus lehmannii		Bushy Yate	419
Eucalyptus polyanthemos		Red Box Gum	420
Eucalyptus pulverulenta		Dollar Leaf Gum	421
Eucalyptus sideroxylon 'Rosea'		Red Iron Bark Gum	422
Eucalyptus viminalis		Ribbon Gum	423
Eugenia myrtifolia	U-jean-e-a	Brush Cherry	291
Eugenia myrtifolia 'Compacta'		Dwarf Brush Cherry	161
Euonymus alata	Eu-on-i-mus	Winged Burning Bush	162
Euonymus japonica		Evergreen Euonymus	163
Euonymus japonica 'Aureo-marginata'		Golden Euonymus	164
Euonymus japonica 'Aureo-variegata'		Gold Spot Euonymus	165
Euonymus japonica 'Silver Queen'		Silver Queen Euonymus	166
Euryops pectinatus	Uri-ops	Euryops	48
Fagus sylvatica	Fa-gus	European Beech	424
Fagus sylvatica 'Atropunicea'		Copper Beech	425
Fagus sylvatica 'Tricolor'		Tricolor Beech	426
Fatshedera lizei	Fat-sa-hed-ra	Botanical Wonder	541
Fatsia japonica see *Aralia sieboldii*			
Fatsia japonica × *Hedera helix* see *Fatshedera lizei*			
Feijoa sellowiana	Fe-hoy-a	Pineapple Guava	292
Ferns			167–182
Adiantum pedatum	Ad-i-an-tum	Five Finger Fern	167
Alsophila australis	Al-sof-il-a	Australian Tree Fern	168
Asparagus densiflorus 'Meyers'	As-par-a-gus	Meyeri	169
Asparagus densiflorus 'Sprengeri'		Sprengeri	170
Aspidium capense	As-pid-i-um	Leather Leaf Fern	171

BOTANIC NAME	PRONUNCIATION	COMMON NAME	PLATE NUMBER
Asplenium bulbiferum	As-plee-ni-um	Mother Fern	172
Cyrtomium falcatum	Ser-to-mi-um	Holly Fern	173
Dicksonia antarctica	Dick-so-ne-a	Tasmanian Tree Fern	174
Nephrolepis exaltata	Ne-fro-lep-is	Boston Sword Fern	175
Pellaea rotundifolia	Pel-lee-a	Round Leaf Fern	176
Platycerium alcicorne	Plat-i-se-ri-um	Staghorn Fern	177
Platycerium grande		Staghorn Fern	178
Polystichum angulare	Po-lis-ti-kum	Single Mother Fern	179
Polystichum munitum		Western Sword Fern	180
Polystichum setosum		Japanese Lace Fern	181
Woodwardia chamissoi	Wood-war-di-a	Giant Chain Fern	182
Festuca glauca	Fes-tu-ka	Blue Fescue	49
Ficus benjamina	Fi-kus	Weeping Fig	293/427
Ficus elastica 'Decora'		Rubber Tree	294/428
Ficus microcarpa nitida see F. retusa nitida			
Ficus pumila see F. repens			
Ficus repens		Creeping Fig	542
Ficus retusa nitida		Indian Laurel	295/429
Flowering Cherry see Prunus			
Flowering Crab Apple see Malus			
Flowering Peach see Prunus			
Flowering Plum see Prunus			
Forsythia Intermedia	For-sith-i-a	Forsythia	185
Fraxinus uhdei	Frax-in-us	Shamel Ash	430
Fraxinus velutina 'Glabra'		Modesto Ash	431
Fremontia californica	Fre-mon-ti-a	Flannel Bush	296
Fremontodendron californicum see Fremontia californica			
Fuchsias	Few-Sha	Fuchsia	183–184I
Gardenia jasminoides 'Mystery'	Gar-de-ni-a	Mystery Cape Jasmine	50
Gardenia jasminoides 'Radicans'		Miniature or Trailing Jasmine	51
Gardenia jasminoides 'Veitchii'		Veitch Jasmine	52
Garrya elliptica	Gar-ri-a	Coast Silk Tassel	186
Gaultheria procumbens	Gaul-ther-i-a	Wintergreen	53
Gaultheria shallon		Salal; Lemonleaf	54
Gelsemium sempervirens	Jel-se-mi-um	Carolina Jessamine	543
Genista racemosa	Jen-is-ta	Sweet Broom	187
Ginkgo biloba	Gink-go	Maidenhair Tree	432
Gleditsia triacanthos inermis	Gle-dit-si-a	Honey Locust	433
Gleditsia triacanthos 'Moraine'		Moraine Locust	434
Gleditsia triacanthos 'Shademaster'		Shademaster Locust	435
Gleditsia triacanthos 'Sunburst'		Sunburst Locust	436
Grevillea 'Noell'	Gre-vil-e-a	Noelli	55
Grevillea robusta		Silk Oak	437
Grewia caffra	Grew-e-a	Lavender Starflower	297
Griselinia littoralis	Gri-se-lin-ia	Kupuka Tree	298

BOTANIC NAME	PRONUNCIATION	COMMON NAME	PLATE NUMBER
Gunnera chilensis	Gun-er-a	Gunnera	188
Hakea suaveolens	Ha-ke-a	Sweet Hakea	299
Harpephyllum caffrum	Harp-a-phil-e-um	Kaffir Plum	438
Hebe buxifolia	He-be	Veronica buxifolia	56
Hebe 'Co-ed'		Veronica 'Co-ed'	57
Hebe 'Evansi'		Veronica rubra	58
Hebe imperialis		Veronica imperialis	59
Hebe menziesii		Veronica menziesii	60
Hebe 'Patty's Purple'		Veronica 'Patty's Purple'	61
Hebe rubra see *Hebe* 'Evansi'			
Hedera canariensis	Hed-ra	Algerian Ivy	544
Hedera helix		English Ivy	545
Hedera helix 'Hahnsii'		Hahn's Ivy	546
Helleborus lividus corsicus	Hel-le-bor-us	Corsican Hellebore	62
Heteromeles arbutifolia see *Photinia arbutifolia*			
Hibbertia scandens see *H. volubilis*			
Hibbertia volubilis	Hi-ber-ti-a	Guinea Gold Vine	547
Hibiscus	Hi-bis-kus		189–190I
Hibiscus syriacus see *Althaea syriaca*			
Hydrangea macrophylla	Hy-dran-je-a	*Hydrangea*	191/192
Hydrangea paniculata 'Grandiflora'		Peegee Hydrangea	300
Hymenosporum flavum	Hi-men-os-por-um	Sweetshade	439
Hypericum beanii see *H. patulum henryi*			
Hypericum calycinum	Hi-per-e-kum	Aaron's Beard	63
Hypericum moseranum		Gold Flower	64
Hypericum patulum henryi		St. John's Wort	65
Ilex altaclarensis 'Wilsonii'	I-lex	Wilson Holly	301/440
Ilex aquifolium		English Holly	302
Ilex aquifolium 'Variegata'		Variegated English Holly	303
Ilex cornuta 'Burfordii'		Burford Holly	193
Ilex cornuta 'Rotunda'		Dwarf Chinese Holly	66
Ilex crenata 'Green Island'		Green Island Holly	67
Jacaranda mimosifolia	Jak-a-ran-da	Jacaranda	441
Jasminum magnificum	Jas-min	Angel Wing Jasmine	68/548
Jasminum mesnyi see *J. primulinum*			
Jasminum nitidum see *J. magnificum*			
Jasminum polyanthum		Pink Jasmine	549
Jasminum primulinum		Primrose Jasmine	550
Juniperus chinensis 'Armstrongii'	Ju-nip-er-us	Armstrong Juniper	602
Juniperus chinensis 'Armstrongii Coasti'		Coasti Juniper	603
Juniperus chinensis 'Blaauw'		Blaauw's Juniper	604
Juniperus chinensis 'Blue Point'		Blue Point Juniper	605
Juniperus chinensis 'Hetzi Glauca'		Hetzi Blue Juniper	606
Juniperus chinensis 'Kaizuka' see *J. c.* 'Torulosa'			
Juniperus chinensis 'Pfitzerana'		Pfitzer Juniper	607

BOTANIC NAME	PRONUNCIATION	COMMON NAME	PLATE NUMBER
Juniperus chinensis 'Pfitzerana Aurea'		Golden Pfitzer Juniper	608
Juniperus chinensis 'Pfitzerana Glauca'		Blue Pfitzer Juniper	609
Juniperus chinensis 'Procumbens'		Japanese Garden Juniper	610
Juniperus chinensis 'Procumbens Nana'		Compact Japanese Garden Juniper	611
Juniperus chinensis 'Robust Green'		Robust Juniper	612
Juniperus chinensis 'San Jose'		San Jose Juniper	613
Juniperus chinensis 'Sea Green'		Sea Green Juniper	614
Juniperus chinensis 'Torulosa'		Hollywood Juniper	615
Juniperus communis 'Stricta'		Irish Juniper	616
Juniperus conferta 'Blue Pacific'		Shore Juniper	617
Juniperus horizontalis		Creeping Juniper	618
Juniperus horizontalis 'Bar Harbor'		Bar Harbor Juniper	619
Juniperus horizontalis 'Variegata'		Variegated Creeping Juniper	620
Juniperus horizontalis 'Wiltonii'		Blue Carpet Juniper	621
Juniperus sabina 'Arcadia'		Arcadia Juniper	622
Juniperus sabina 'Broadmoor'		Broadmoor Juniper	623
Juniperus sabina Buffalo'		Buffalo Juniper	624
Juniperus sabina 'Tamariscifolia'		Tamarix or Tam Juniper	625
Juniperus scopulorum 'Blue Heaven'		Blue Heaven Juniper	626
Juniperus scopulorum 'Pathfinder'		Pathfinder Juniper	627
Juniperus squamata 'Meyeri'		Meyer Juniper	628
Juniperus virginana 'Silver Spreader'		Silver Spreader Juniper	629
Justicia brandegeana see *Beloperone guttata*			
Kalmia latifolia	Kal-mi-a	Mountain Laurel	194
Kerria japonica	Ker-i-a	Japanese Kerria	195
Koelreuteria bipinnata	Kol-ro-te-ri-a	Chinese Flame Tree	**442**
Koelreuteria paniculata		Golden Rain Tree	**443**
Kolkwitzia amabilis	Kol-kwit-zi-a	Beauty Bush	304
Laburnum watereri 'Vossii'	La-ber-num	Golden Chain Tree	445
Lagerstroemia indica	La-gur-stre-mi-a	Crape Myrtle	305
Lagunaria pattersonii	La-gun-ar-i-a	Cow Itch Tree	306
Lantana camara	Lan-tan-a	Lantana	196/197
Lantana montevidensis see *L. sellowiana*			
Lantana sellowiana		Trailing Lantana	69
Laurus nobilis	Lau-rus	Grecian Laurel; Grecian Bay	307
Lavandula angustifolia see *L. vera*			
Lavandula vera	La-van-du-la	English Lavender	70
Leptospermum laevigatum	Lep-to-sper-mum	Australian Tea Tree	308
Leptospermum laevigatum 'Reevesii'		Dwarf Australian Tea Tree	198
Leptospermum scoparium 'Helene Strybing'		Flowering Tea Tree	199
Leptospermum scoparium 'Keatleyi'		Pink Flowering Tea Tree	309
Leptospermum scoparium 'Ruby Glow'		Red Flowering Tea Tree	200
Leptospermum scoparium 'Snow White'		White Flowering Tea Tree	71
Leucodendron argenteum	Lu-ko-den-dron	Silver Tree	310
Leucophyllum frutescens	Lu-ko-fi-lum	Texas Sage; Senisa	201

BOTANIC NAME	PRONUNCIATION	COMMON NAME	PLATE NUMBER
Leucothoe catesbaei 'Rainbow'	Lu-koth-o-e	Drooping Leucothoe	72
Leucothoe fontanesiana see *L. catesbaei* 'Rainbow'			
Libocedrus decurrens	Li-bo-se-drus	Incense Cedar	630
Ligustrum japonicum	Li-gus-trum	Japanese Privet	446
Ligustrum japonicum		Wax Leaf Privet	202
Ligustrum ovalifolium		California Privet	203
Lippia citriodora	Lip-pia	Lemon Verbena	204
Liquidambar styraciflua	Lik-wid-am-ber	American Sweet Gum	447
Liquidambar styraciflua 'Burgundy'		American Sweet Gum	448
Liquidambar styraciflua 'Palo Alto'		American Sweet Gum	449
Liriodendron tulipifera	Lir-i-o-den-dron	Tulip Tree	450
Liriope muscari	Li-ri-o-pe	Lily Turfs	73
Lonicera hildebrandiana	Lon-is-era	Giant Burmese Honeysuckle	551
Lonicera japonica 'Halliana'		Honeysuckle	552
Loropetalum chinense	Lor-o-pet-a-lum		74
Lyonothamnus floribundus	Lyn-o-tha-mus	Catalina Ironwood	451
Magnolia (Deciduous Varieties)	Mag-no-lia	Tulip Trees	311–311K
Magnolia grandiflora		Southern Magnolia	451
Magnolia grandiflora 'Russet'		Russet Magnolia	452
Magnolia grandiflora 'St. Mary'		St. Mary's Magnolia	453
Magnolia grandiflora 'Samuel Sommer'		Samuel Sommer Magnolia	454
Mahonia aquifolium	Ma-ho-nia	Oregon Grape	205
Mahonia aquifolium 'Compacta'		Dwarf Oregon Grape	75
Mahonia bealei		Siberian Grape	206
Mahonia lomariifolia		Chinese Holly Grape	207
Mahonia nervosa		Longleaf Mahonia	76
Mahonia pinnata		California Holly Grape	208
Malus (In Variety)	Mal-us	Flowering Crab Apple	455–465
Mandevilla 'Alice du Pont'	Man-de-vil-a	Chile Jasmine	553
Maytenus boaria	May-ten-us	Mayten Tree	466
Melaleuca decussata	Mel-a-lu-ka	Lilac Melaleuca	312
Melaleuca leucadendra		Swamp Tea Tree	467
Melaleuca linariifolia		Flaxleaf Paperbark	468
Melia azedarach 'Umbraculiformis'	Me-li-a	Texas Umbrella Tree	469
Melianthus major	Mel-i-an-thus	Honey Bush	209
Metasequoia glyprostroboides	Met-a-se-kwoi-a	Dawn Redwood	631
Metrosideros excelsus see *M. tomentosa*			
Metrosideros tomentosa	Me-tro-si-de-ros	New Zealand Christmas Tree	470
Michelia figo see *M. fuscata*			
Michelia fuscata	Mi-ke-li-a	Banana Shrub	210
Moraea iridioides	Mo-ree-a	Butterfly Iris	77
Morus alba 'Fruitless'	Mor-us	Fruitless Mulberry	471
Murraya exotica	Mur-re-a	Orange Jessamine	211
Murraya paniculata see *M. exotica*			
Musa ensete	Mu-sa	Banana Tree	313

BOTANIC NAME	PRONUNCIATION	COMMON NAME	PLATE NUMBER
Musa maurelii		Red Leaf or Ethiopian Banana	314
Myoporum laetum	My-o-por-um		315/472
Myrsine africana	Mer-seen	African Box	212
Myrtus communis	Mer-tus	Common Myrtle	213
Myrtus communis 'Compacta'		Dwarf Myrtle	78
Myrtus ugni		Chilean Guava	79
Nandina domestica	Nan-dy-na	Heavenly Bamboo	214
Nandina domestica 'Nana Compacta'		Dwarf Heavenly Bamboo	80
Nephrolepis exaltata	Ne-fro-lep-is	Boston Sword Fern	175
Nerium oleander	Nee-ri-um	Oleander	215–217
Olea europeae 'Mission'	O-le-a	Mission Olive	473
Osmanthus delavayi	Os-man-thus	Delavayi Osmanthus	218
Osmanthus fortunei		Fortunei Osmanthus	316
Osmanthus fragrans		Sweet Olive	219
Osmanthus heterophyllus see *O. ilicifolius*			
Osmanthus ilicifolius		False Holly	220
Osmanthus ilicifolius 'Variegatus'		Variegated False Holly	221
Oxydendrum arboreum	Ox-i-den-drum	Sourwood or Sorrel Tree	474
Pachysandra terminalis	Pak-i-san-dra	Japanese Spurge	81
Palms			317–330
Parthenocissus see *Ampelopsis*			
Passiflora alatocaerulea see *P. pfordtii*			
Passiflora jamesonii	Pas-si-flora	Pink Passion Vine	554
Passiflora pfordtii		Passion Vine	555
Pellaea rotundifolia	Pel-lee-a	Round Leaf Fern	176
Pernettya mucronata	Pur-net-tia	Pernettya	82
Philadelphus virginalis	Phil-a-del-fus	Mock Orange	222
Philodendron 'Evansii'	Phil-o-den-dron	Outdoor Philodendron	223
Philodendron selloum		Split Leaf Philodendron	224
Phoenix canariensis	Fe-niks	Canary Island Date Palm	324
Phoenix reclinata		Senegal Date Palm	325
Phoenix roebelenii		Pygmy Date Palm	326
Phormium tenax	For-mi-um	New Zealand Flax	225
Photinia arbutifolia	Foh-tin-i-a	California Toyon	331
Photinia fraseri		Fraser Photinia	332/475
Photinia serrulata		Chinese Photinia	333
Phyllostachys see *Bambusa phyllostachys*			
Picea abies see *P. excelsa*			
Picea excelsa	Pi-se-a	Norway Spruce	632
Picea excelsa 'Nidiformis'		Nest Spruce	633
Picea excelsa 'Pendula'		Weeping Norway Spruce	634
Picea excelsa 'Pygmaea'		Dwarf Norway Spruce	635
Picea glauca 'Conica'		Dwarf Alberta Spruce	636
Picea pungens		Colorado Spruce	637
Picea pungens 'Koster'		Koster Blue Spruce	638
Picea pungens 'Moerheimii'		Moerheim Spruce	639

BOTANIC NAME	PRONUNCIATION	COMMON NAME	PLATE NUMBER
Pieris formosa forrestii	Py-er-is	Chinese Andromeda	227
Pieris forrestii see *P. formosa forrestii*			
Pieris japonica		Lily-of-the-Valley Shrub	228
Pieris japonica 'Flame of the Forest'		Flame of the Forest	229
Pieris japonica 'Flamingo Pink'		Pink Lily-of-the-Valley Shrub	230
Pieris japonica 'Variegata'		Variegated Lily-of-the-Valley Shrub	231
Pinus aristata	Py-nus	Bristlecone Pine	640
Pinus canariensis		Canary Island Pine	641
Pinus densiflora 'Umbraculifera'		Tanyosho or Table Mountain Pine	642
Pinus halepensis		Aleppo Pine	643
Pinus mugo		Mugho Pine	644
Pinus nigra		Austrian Black Pine	645
Pinus patula		Jelecote or Mexican Pine	646
Pinus pinea		Italian Stone Pine	647
Pinus radiata		Monterey Pine	648
Pinus strobus 'Nana'		Dwarf White Pine	649
Pinus sylvestris		Scotch Pine	650
Pinus sylvestris 'Fastigiata'		Erect Scotch Pine	651
Pinus thunbergiana		Japanese Black Pine	652/653
Pistacia chinensis	Pis-ta-shi-a	Chinese Pistache	476
Pittosporum crassifolium	Pit-tos-por-um	Karo Pittosporum	334
Pittosporum eugenioides		Tarata Pittosporum	335
Pittosporum phillyraeoides		Desert Willow	336
Pittosporum rhombifolium		Diamond Leaf Pittosporum	337
Pittosporum tenuifolium		Tawhiwhi	338
Pittosporum tobira		Japanese Pittosporum	232
Pittosporum tobira 'Variegata'		Japanese Variegated Pittosporum	233
Pittosporum tobira 'Wheelerii'		Wheeler's Dwarf Pittosporum	83
Pittosporum undulatum		Victorian Box	339/477
Platanus acerifolia	Plat-a-nus	European Sycamore or London Plane	478
Platanus occidentalis		American Sycamore	479
Platanus racemosa		California Sycamore	480
Platycerium alcicorna	Plat-i-se-ri-um	Staghorn Fern	177
Platycerium grande		Staghorn Fern	178
Platycladus orientalis see *Thuja orientalis*			
Pleroma splendens	Ple-ro-ma	Princess Flower	340
Plumbago auriculata see *P. capensis*			
Plumbago capensis	Plum-ba-go	Cape Plumbago	234
Podocarpus gracilior	Pod-o-kar-pus	Fern Pine	341/481/654
Podocarpus macrophyllus		Yew Pine	342/655
Podocarpus macrophyllus maki		Shrubby Yew	343/656
Poinciana gilliesii	Poin-si-a-na	Bird of Paradise Shrub	235
Polygala dalmaisiana	Po-lig-a-la	Sweet Pea Shrub	84

BOTANIC NAME	PRONUNCIATION	COMMON NAME	PLATE NUMBER
Polygonum aubertii	Po-lig-o-num	Silver Lace Vine	556
Polystichum angulare	Po-lis-ti-kum	Single Mother Fern	179
Polystichum munitum		Western Sword Fern	180
Polystichum setosum		Japanese Lace Fern	181
Populus nigra 'Italica'	Pop-u-lus	Lombardy Poplar	482
Potentilla fruticosa var. 'Katherine Dykes'	Poh-ten-til-la	Cinquefoil	85
Prunus caroliniana	Pru-nus	Carolina Laurel Cherry	344
Prunus caroliniana 'Compacta'		Dwarf Carolina Laurel Cherry	236
Prunus cerasifera		Flowering Plum	483–487
Prunus glandulosa		Dwarf Flowering Almond	86
Prunus ilicifolia		Holly Leaf Cherry	345
Prunus laurocerasus		English Laurel	346
Prunus laurocerasus 'Otto Luyken'		Luykens Laurel	87
Prunus laurocerasus 'Zabeliana'		Zabel Laurel	88
Prunus lusitanica		Portugal Laurel	347
Prunus lyonii		Catalina Cherry	348
Prunus persica		Flowering Peach	488–490
Prunus serrulata		Flowering Cherry	491–496
Prunus subhirtella		Flowering Cherry	498–499A
Prunus yedoensis		Flowering Cherry	497
Pseudotsuga menziesii see *P. taxifolia*			
Pseudotsuga taxifolia	Su-do-su-ga	Douglas Fir	657
Psidium cattleianum	Sid-i-um	Red Strawberry Guava	349
Psidium littorale longipes see *P. cattleianum*			
Punica granatum	Peu-ni-ka	Pomegranate	350
Punica granatum 'Nana'		Dwarf Pomegranate	89
Pyracantha coccinea 'Lalandei'	Py-rah-kan-tha	Firethorn	351
Pyracantha fortuneana 'Graberi'		Firethorn	237
Pyracantha 'Santa Cruz'		Santa Cruz Firethorn	90
Pyrostegia venusta see *Bignonia venusta*			
Pyrus calleryana 'Bradfordi'	Pyr-us	Bradford Pear	500
Pyrus kawakamii		Evergreen Pear	501
Quercus agrifolia	Quer-kus	California Live Oak	502
Quercus coccinea		Scarlet Oak	503
Quercus ilex		Holly Oak	504
Quercus palustris		Pin Oak	505
Quercus suber		Cork Oak	506
Raphiolepis indica 'Ballerina'	Raf-i-ol-e-pis	Raphiolepis 'Ballerina'	91
Raphiolepis indica 'Clara'		Raphiolepis 'Clara'	92
Raphiolepis indica 'Enchantress'		Raphiolepis 'Enchantress'	93
Raphiolepis indica 'Pink Lady'		Raphiolepis 'Pink Lady'	94
Raphiolepis indica 'Rosea'		Raphiolepis 'Rosea'	95
Raphiolepis indica 'Springtime'		Raphiolepis 'Springtime'	96
Raphiolepis ovata			238
Raphiolepis umbellata see *R. ovata*			
Rhamnus alaternus	Ram-nus	Italian Buckthorn	352

BOTANIC NAME	PRONUNCIATION	COMMON NAME	PLATE NUMBER
Rhamnus alaternus 'Variegata'		Variegated Italian Buckthorn	353
Rhamnus californica		California Coffee Berry	239
Rhapis excelsa	Ray-fis	Lady Palm	327
Rhododendrons	Rho-do-den-dron	Rhododendron	240
Rhoicissus capensis see *Cissus capensis*			
Rhus integrifolia	Roos	Lemonade Berry	354
Rhus ovata		Sugar Bush	241
Rhus typhina 'Laciniata'		Staghorn Sumac	242
Rhynchospermum jasminioides	Rink-co-sper-mum	Star Jasmine	97/557
Ribes sanguineum	Ri-beez	Red Flowering Currant	243
Ribes speciosum		Fuchsia Flowering Gooseberry	98
Ribes viburnifolium		Evergreen Currant	99
Robinia pseudoacacia 'Decaisneana'	Ro-bin-i-a	Pink Locust	507
Romneya coulteri	Rom-ni-a	Matilija Poppy	244
Rosa banksiae 'Lutea'	Roh-za	Yellow Banksia Rose	558
Rosmarinus officinalis	Ros-ma-ri-nus	Rosemary	100
Rosmarinus officinalis 'Prostrata'		Trailing Rosemary	101
Salix babylonica	Say-lix	Weeping Willow	508
Salix matsudana 'Tortuosa'		Corkscrew Willow	509
Sarcococca hookerana humilis	Sar-ko-coke-ah	Small Hookeri	102
Sarcococca ruscifolia		Fragrant Sarcococca	245
Saxifraga rubicunda	Sax-si-fray-ga	Saxifrage	103
Schinus molle	Shinus	California Pepper Tree	510
Schinus terebinthifolius		Brazilian Pepper Tree	511
Sciadopitys verticillata	Ski-a-dop-i-tis	Umbrella Pine	658
Seaforthia elegans	Se-for-thi-a	King Palm	328
Senecio greyi	Sen-ee-si-o	Senecio	104
Sequoiadendron giganteum see *Sequoia gigantea*			
Sequoia gigantea	Se-kwoi-a	Giant Sequoia	659
Sequoia gigantea 'Pendulum'		Weeping Giant Sequoia	660
Sequoia sempervirens		Coast Redwood	661
Sesbania tripetii see *Daubentonia tripetii*			
Skimmia japonica	*Skim-i-a*	*Skimmia*	105–105A
Solandra guttata	So-lan-dra	Cup of Gold Vine	559
Solandra maxima see *S. guttata*			
Solanum jasminoides	So-la-num	Potato Vine	560
Solanum rantonnetii		Paraguay Nightshade	561
Sollya heterophylla	Sol-li-a	Australian Bluebell Creeper	106
Sorbus aucuparia	Sor-bus	European Mountain Ash	512
Spartium junceum	Spar-ti-um	Yellow Spanish Broom	246
Sphaeropteris cooperi see *Alsophila australis*			
Spiraea prunifolia	Spi-re-a	Shoe Button Spiraea; Bridal Wreath	247
Spiraea vanhouttei			248
Stenocarpus sinuatus	Sten-o-car-pus	Firewheel Tree	513
Stephanotis floribunda	Stef-a-no-tis	Madagascar Jasmine	562

BOTANIC NAME	PRONUNCIATION	COMMON NAME	PLATE NUMBER
Sterculia diversifolia	Stur-cu-lia	Bottle Tree	514
Stranvaesia davidiana	Stran-ve-zi-a	Chinese Stranvaesia	355
Strelitzia nicolai	Stre-lit-si-a	Giant Bird of Paradise	356
Strelitzia reginae		Bird of Paradise	107
Syringa laciniata see *S. persica laciniata*			
Syringa persica laciniata	Si-ring-a	Cut-leaf Persian Lilac	249
Syringa vulgaris		Common Lilac	250–253
Syzygium paniculata see *Eugenia myrtifolia*			
Syzygium paniculatum 'Compacta' see *Eugenia myrtifolia* 'Compacta'			
Tamarix parviflora see *T. tetrandra*			
Tamarix tetrandra	Tam-a-riks	Tamarisk	357
Taxus baccata	Tax-us	English Yew	662
Taxus baccata 'Fastigiata'		Irish Yew	663
Taxus baccata 'Fastigiata Aurea'		Golden Irish Yew	664
Taxus baccata 'Repandens'		Spreading English Yew	665
Taxus baccata 'Repandens Aurea'		Golden Spreading English Yew	666
Tecoma capensis	Te-koh-ma	Cape Honeysuckle	358/563
Tecomaria capensis see *Tecoma capensis*			
Ternstroemia gymnanthera see *T. japonica*			
Ternstroemia japonica	Tern-strom-e-a	Ternstroemia	254
Teucrium chamaedrys	Teu-kre-um	Dwarf Germander	108
Teucrium fruticans		Bush Germander	255
Thuja occidentalis 'Little Gem'	Theu-ja	Green Globe Arborvitae	667
Thuja occidentalis 'Pyramidalis'		Pyramidal Arborvitae	668
Thuja occidentalis 'Woodwardii'		Woodward Arborvitae	669
Thuja orientalis 'Aurea Nana'		Dwarf Golden Arborvitae	670
Thuja orientalis 'Beverleyensis'		Beverly Hills Arborvitae	671
Tibouchina urvilleana see *Pleroma splendens*			
Tilia cordata	Til-i-a	Small Leafed Linden	515
Trachelospermum jasminoides see *Rhynchospermum jasminoides*			
Trachycarpus fortunei see *Chamaerops excelsa*			
Tristania conferta	Tris-ta-nia	Brisbane Box	516
Tristania laurina		Kanooka Box	517
Tupidanthus calyptratus	Tup-i-dan-thus	Umbrella Tree	359
Tsuga canadensis	Tsu-ga	Canadian Hemlock	672
Tsuga canadensis 'Pendula'		Weeping Hemlock	673
Ungi molinae see *Myrtus ugni*			
Ulmus glabra 'Camperdownii'	Ul-mus	Camperdown Elm	518
Ulmus parvifolia		Evergreen Elm	519
Ulmus parvifolia 'Brea'		Chinese Evergreen Elm	520
Vaccinium ovatum	Vak-sin-i-um	Evergreen Huckleberry	256
Veronica see *Hebe*			
Viburnum burkwoodii	Vi-ber-num	Burkwood Viburnum	360
Viburnum davidii		David Viburnum	109

BOTANIC NAME	PRONUNCIATION	COMMON NAME	PLATE NUMBER
Viburnum japonicum		Japanese Viburnum	361
Viburnum macrocephalum 'Sterile'		Chinese Snowball	362
Viburnum odoratissimum		Sweet Viburnum	363
Viburnum opulus 'Roseum'		Snowball	364
Viburnum suspensum		Sandankwa Viburnum	257
Viburnum tinus 'Robustum'		Roundleaf Laurustinus	365
Washingtonia filifera	Wash-ing-to-nia	California Fan Palm	329
Washingtonia robusta		Mexican Fan Palm	330
Weigela florida 'Bristol Ruby'	Wi-ge-la	Red Weigela	258
Weigela florida 'Rosea'		Pink Weigela	259
Westringia rosmariniformis	West-ring-ga	Australian Rosemary	110
Wisteria	Wis-ta-ri-a	Wisteria	563–568
Woodwardia chamissoi	Wood-war-di-a	Giant Chain Fern	182
Woodwardia fimbriata see *W. chamissoi*			
Xylosma congestum see *X. senticosum*			
Xylosma senticosum	Zi-los-ma	Shiny Xylosma	260
Yucca aloifolia	Yuk-a	Spanish Bayonet	366
Yucca gloriosa		Spanish Dagger	367
Yucca recurvifolia		Spineless Yucca	368
Zelkova serrata	Zel-ko-va	Sawleaf Zelkova	521

LOW-GROWING SHRUBS

Plants in this section seldom reach more than 4 ft and are easily kept
under that height. All are evergreen unless otherwise mentioned.

1   Acanthus mollis

Acanthus mollis   Zone 8

(Bear's Breech)

1   Huge, notched, dark green leaves often 2 ft long. The leaves grow
directly out of the ground, like a perennial, rather than a shrub. Rigid,
erect, 3 ft flower spikes with whitish or purple-tinged flowers in May
and June. Very tropical looking. Stands abuse. Best grown in semi-
shade where roots can be confined as they travel underground and are
hard to eradicate. The old leaves should be cut to the ground as soon as
it finishes blooming.   Planting Group 1

2   Acer palmatum 'Dissectum'

Acer palmatum 'Dissectum'   Zone 5

2   Deciduous foliage comes out red then turns to a rusty green in
summer. Shade in warmer areas but will grow in the sun when the
roots are kept shaded and moist but will not tolerate wind. Requires a
regular watering schedule.   Planting Group 5

> *Acer palmatum* 'Dissectum' is listed among low-growing plants
> as it is seldom grown more than 4 ft tall. However the above
> plant, now about 100 years old and with ideal conditions, is 10
> ft. Given time and excellent conditions, most plants will grow
> taller than expected.

3   Acer palmatum 'Dissectum Ever Red'

Acer palmatum 'Dissectum Ever Red'   Zone 5

3   Deciduous. Same weeping form as *A. p.* 'Dissectum', except this
holds its beautiful, deep red color throughout the summer if regularly
watered and kept away from wind.   Planting Group 5

4   Acer palmatum 'Dissectum Viridis'

Acer palmatum 'Dissectum Viridis'   Zone 5

(Japanese Green Lace Leaf Maple)

4   Deciduous foliage and form the same as *A. p.* 'Dissectum', except it
stays bright apple green throughout the summer. Requires regular
water and more shade than other varieties of *A. palmatum* and no
wind.   Planting Group 5

5   *Agapanthus africanus*

6   *Agapanthus africanus* 'Peter Pan'

Agapanthus africanus   Zone 8
(Blue Lily of the Nile)

5   A hardy perennial, producing dense masses of dark green, amaryllis-like leaves, and bearing clusters of lovely blue flowers on tall, naked stalks in the summer. Will stand the "impossible" location in full sun. A white form, *A. a.* 'Alba' is also available. Deer proof.
      Planting Group 1

7   *Agave attenuata*

Agave attenuata   Zone 9

7   Huge rosette of large, thick, fleshy, gray-green leaves. From the succulent family and tropical in effect with very unusual flowers.
      Planting Group 1

Agapanthus africanus 'Peter Pan'   Zone 8

6   Excellent, dwarf form of the popular "Lily of the Nile," with small clusters of blue flowers on stems about 12 in. tall. There is also a dwarf white form. Deer proof.   Planting Group 1

8   *Andromeda polifolia*

Andromeda polifolia   Zone 2
(Bog Andromeda or Bog Rosemary)

8   Dwarf evergreen shrublet to 10 in. with gray-green foliage and covered with pink blossoms in the spring. Needs a well-drained but moist place in your garden and with an acid-soil situation. Best in coastal Northern California or in the Northwest.   Planting Group 1

Arctostaphylos densiflora 'Howard McMinn'   Zone 9

9   Leaves are small, ½–1 in., and light to dark glossy green. Flowers are whitish-pink. Will grow to about 30 in. high with a 6 ft spread. Best planted with afternoon shade or an eastern exposure. Tip prune after blooming for tight, dense growth. Needs a well-drained location and do not water too much. Deer proof.   Planting Group 3

10   Arctostaphylos hookeri

Arctostaphylos hookeri   Zone 7
(Monterey Manzanita)

10   Grows to about 2 ft with a 4–5 ft spread. Leaves are shiny bright green; pinkish flowers. Excellent cover for dry slopes. Deer proof.   Planting Group 2

9   Arctostaphylos densiflora 'Howard McMinn'

11   Arctostaphylos uva ursi

Arctostaphylos uva ursi   Zone 2
(Kinnikinnick or Bear Berry)

11   A creeping Manzanita with rich green leaves that grow only a few inches high. The plants take root as they spread. Should be planted at about 3 ft centers. Flowers are white followed by red berries. Widely planted, especially near the coast and in the Northwest.   Planting Group 2

Aspidistra elatior   Zone 9
(Cast Iron Plant)

12   Excellent both in a tub (or indoors) or planted in the garden as a specimen. One of the most rugged plants for a tough, dark location. Very good as an indoor specimen.   Planting Group 5

12   Aspidistra elatior

AZALEAS

Now referred to by botanists as Rhododendrons. However, in this book, we are calling them Azaleas because this is the way they are described in the wholesale nursery catalogues. They are unsurpassed for blooms in winter and spring. They are all lovers of acid soil and do best when planted in peat moss or leaf mold with excellent drainage. They all like partial shade or morning sun and plenty of water, however, the *Southern Indicas* will grow in full sun if they do not receive reflected heat. Feed as soon as the blooming is over and while the plant is in active growth. Prune, even with hedge shears, in May or June to shape the plant for compact growth.

All Planting Group 5

Southern Indicas (Hardy to about 25°)   Zone 9
  'Brilliant'   single red
  'Duc de Rohan'   single salmon-pink
  'Fielder's White'   single fragrant white
  'Formosa'   single rich lavender
  'George Lindley Tabor'   large single pink
  'Glory of Sunninghill'   single orange-red
  'L. J. Bobbink'   single pinkish-lavender
  'Pride of Dorking'   single cardinal-red
  'Southern Charm'   single deep rose

Kurumes   Zone 8

The *Kurume* strain blooms in the late spring. The plants are hardier in the garden than the *Indicas,* both to cold and in their capacity to stand more sun. The flowers are not so large as the *Indicas* but are more profuse. Again, dozens of varieties to be found and we only attempt to list a few:
  'Coral Bells'   single bright pink, stands sun
  'Hexe'   deep red hose-in-hose
  'Hino' ('Hinodegiri')   single bright red, stands sun
  'Hino-crimson'   single crimson, stands sun
  'Redwing'   single ruffled, red, large
  'Sherwood Orchid'   single orchid, stands sun
  'SherwoodRed'   single red, stands sun
  'Sweetheart Supreme'   double light pink
  'Ward's Ruby'   single, brilliant dark red

Azaleas for the Shade   Zone 9

Belgian Indicas or closely related varieties best above 25°. The choicest of all the Azaleas. Mostly double flowers in a great range of colors. Listed below are some of the most readily available.

'Alaska'	double white
'Albert and Elizabeth'	double white with pink edging
'Avenir'	double salmon
'Blushing Bride'	large, double soft pink
'California Snow'	large, double white
'California Sunset'	large, double salmon and white variegated
'Chimes'	large, double red
'Dr. Bergmann'	varied shades of pink, rose, and salmon
'Erie' ('Eric Schame')	double variegated pink and white
'Fred Sanders'	large, double rose-red
'Jean Hearrens'	large, double lavender-pink
'Niobe'	large, double pure white
'Orchidiflora'	extra large, double lavender-pink
'Paul Schame'	double coral salmon
'Pearl De Sweynarde'	large, double white
'Picotee'	large, variegated white with pink edge
'Pink Pearl'	large, double delicate pink
'Rose Queen'	hose-in-hose pink
'Vervaeneana Alba'	large, double pure white
'William van Orange'	double orange

13A   *Azalea altaclarensis*

13B   *Azalea Exbury hybrids*

Azalea altaclarensis   Zone 5

(Chinese Azalea)

13A   Deciduous. Resembles *A. mollis,* except in color. This variety has large flowers of apricot-yellow in varying tones and grows to about 6 ft. Same growing instructions as *A. mollis.*   Planting Group 1

Azalea Exbury hybrids   Zone 6

13B   Deciduous. There are many named varieties but, for the most part, nurseries carry seedling plants by color only. Red, orange, pink, and white. These beautiful plants grow in more sun than most other *Azaleas* and are upright in growth to about 5 ft. Should have a loose, sandy, peaty soil that is mounded up around the stems.
Planting Group 1

13C   *Azalea mollis*

If you want to treat your Azaleas right when you plant them, dig a hole 3 ft in diameter and 6 in. deep, even for a one-gallon can size, larger if the plant has a larger root ball. Fill this hole with 75% peat moss and 25% loose loam or compost. In dry weather use a prepared wetting agent once a month, which will force the peat moss to accept water.

Azalea mollis   Zone 6

13C   Deciduous to 6 ft. The flowers, borne in large clusters, are bright orange to flame, also yellow and white. Best grown in full sun on the coast. Partial shade inland in a well-drained, well-watered location. Likes acid soil, so plant with leaf mold and peat moss. The plant does best when planted in a mound like a hill of potatoes, with peat moss and leaf mold mixture.   Planting Group 1

Azalea occidentalis   Zone 7

(Western Azalea)

13D   Deciduous. Has delightful, fragrant, showy, tubed-shaped flowers in rounded clusters. The flowers, borne in May and June, vary in color from white to cream to pinkish. Grows to about 6 ft, but occasionally to 10 ft or more.   Planting Group 4

13D   *Azalea occidentalis*

13E   Azalea 'Sweetheart Supreme'

13F   Azalea 'Mission Bell'

13G   Azalea 'Rose Queen'

13H   Azalea 'Southern Charm'

13I   Azalea 'California Sunset'

13J   Azalea 'Memorie Jean Hearrens'

13K   Azalea 'Erie' ('Eric Schame')

13L   Azalea 'Dr. Bergmann'

13M   Azalea 'Sherwood Red'

13N   Azalea 'Iveryana'

13O Azalea 'Redwing'

13P Azalea 'George Lindley Tabor'

13Q Azalea Garden

13R Azalea 'Ward's Ruby'

13S Azalea 'Coral Bells'

13T Azalea 'Hino-crimson'

13U Azalea 'Ledifolia Rosea'

13V Azalea 'L. J. Bobbink'

13W Azalea 'Mamie'

13X Azalea 'Duc de Rohan'

14   *Bambusa sasa* 'Pygmaea'

15   *Beloperone guttata*

Bambusa sasa 'Pygmaea'   Zone 9
(Dwarf Bamboo)

14   Excellent to use where a low-growing plant or ground cover is
desired but travels and can become a pest. However, planting in a confined area is helpful. Golden-green foliage. Also available in a silver
variegated form.   Planting Group 1

Beloperone guttata (Justicia brandegeana)   Zone 9
(Shrimp Plant)

15   Dwarf shrub with attractive, long, reddish-brown bracts that hide
a small, white flower. Likes heat, takes full sun, but does best in partial
shade with good drainage.   Planting Group 1

16   *Bouvardia* 'Albatross'

Bouvardia 'Albatross' *(B. longiflora)*   Zone 9
(White Bouvardia)

16   A shrub noted for its fragrant, showy clusters of white flowers.
Tender. To develop a nice plant, it is necessary to pick the flowers with
a short stem regularly. Grow in partial shade with mixtures of peat
moss and leaf mold. Use acid fertilizer. Because it is a victim of smog,
not readily available.   Planting Group 5

Buxus japonica (B. microphylla japonica)   Zone 8
(Japanese Boxwood)

17   Popular, quick-growing, low hedge or shrub. Foliage medium to
light green. Usually kept clipped to a height of 2–3 ft, but will grow to 6
ft or more if untrimmed.   Planting Group 1

17   *Buxus japonica*

18   *Buxus sempervirens 'Suffruticosa'*

Buxus sempervirens 'Suffruticosa'   Zone 7
(Dwarf English Boxwood)

18   This "true" dwarf variety is widely used in the Northwest and Northern California. Ideal for a low evergreen border to be kept at 1–2 ft. Requires closer planting than the Japanese Boxwood.
                                                        Planting Group 1

Many varieties of *Calluna vulgaris,* the true Scotch Heather, are grown in the Northwest. We show only two. These are very similar to some of the *Ericas* shown later in this book.

Calluna vulgaris 'H.E. Beale'   Zone 4
(Pink Scotch Heather)

19   A very colorful, loose mound to 2 ft with dark green, needle-like foliage and soft pink double flowers on long spikes which are good for cutting. Needs a well-drained soil.   Planting Group 1

19   *Calluna vulgaris* 'H. E. Beale'

Calluna vulgaris 'Searlei'   Zone 4

20   Another of the many varieties of the Heaths grown on the Pacific Coast, mostly in the Northwest. This one has white flowers and blooms in the late summer and fall in a well-drained area.
                                                        Planting Group 1

20   *Calluna vulgaris* 'Searlei'

21   *Carissa grandiflora* 'Tuttle'

Carissa grandiflora 'Tuttle' (*C. macrocarpa* 'Tuttle')   Zone 9
(Dwarf Natal Plum)

21   This knee-high, dwarf form of *C. grandiflora* has the same lush, green foliage as the parent with abundant white flowers which are followed by red fruit. Excellent ground cover to control unwanted foot traffic; there are just enough thorns.   Planting Group 1

Ceanothus griseus horizontalis   Zone 8
(Carmel Creeper)

23   Very popular in the coastal region. The leaves are bright green and about 2 in. long. The plant is covered in spring with light blue flowers. Plants grow 18–30 in. high, and will cover the ground within a year, if growing conditions are right. For ground cover, should not be planted closer than 5 or 6 ft centers, otherwise the plants will mound up.   Planting Group 2

23   *Ceanothus griseus horizontalis*

22   *Ceanothus gloriosus*

Ceanothus gloriosus   Zone 8
(Point Reyes Creeper)

22   Low-growing, dense mat, usually about 6 or 8 in. high. The foliage is small, spiny, and dark green with medium blue flowers. Very good when planted on top of a wall hanging straight down. One of the best *Ceanothus* ground covers when planted 3–4 ft centers.
                                              Planting Group 2

24   *Ceratostigma plumbaginoides*

Ceratostigma plumbaginoides   Zone 8
(Blue Leadwort)

24   Ground cover plant with intense blue flowers in summer and fall. Looks sad in winter so should be cut back to the ground in late fall. Spreads from underground roots. Will grow in sun on the coast but prefers shade inland. Flowers freely in the shade.   Planting Group 1

Cistus corbariensis (C. hybridus)   Zone 8
(White Rock Rose)

25   Another wonderful cover for dry, sunny slopes either in the desert or right next to the ocean. Plant is very compact and has 2 in., white flowers. Must have dry, well-drained location. Deer proof.
                                              Planting Group 3

26   *Cistus ladanifera maculatus*

Cistus ladanifera maculatus   Zone 8
(Crimson Spot Rock Rose)

26   Compact growth to 3 ft high with glossy green leaves and 3 in., white flowers with a crimson spot on each petal. Flowers heavily in June and July. Will stand salt spray or hot desert and enjoys poor soil. Will also stand drought conditions and is an excellent bank cover. Deer proof.   Planting Group 3

25   *Cistus corbariensis*

27   Cistus purpureus

28   Clivia miniata

Cistus purpureus   Zone 8

(Orchid Spot Rock Rose)

27   Compact growth up to 4 or 5 ft with dark green foliage. Flowers are orchid with a dark eye. Enjoys drought, poor soil, ocean breeze, but is equally at home in the hot country. Deer proof.   Planting Group 2

Clivia miniata   Zone 9

(Kafir Lily)

28   Large, deep green, Lily-like shaped leaves. Bright orange flower clusters in late winter or early spring. Needs shade and no direct sun. Excellent tub plant for shade as it likes confinement.

Planting Group 5

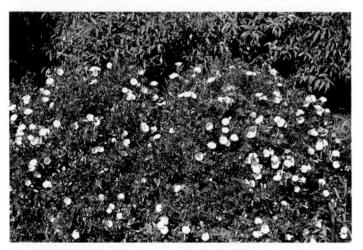

29   Convolvulus cneorum

Convolvulus cneorum   Zone 9

(Bush Morning Glory)

29   A very nice, low-growing, silver-gray plant that should be planted in full sun. Tends to be leggy in the shade; white flowers similar to Morning Glory (it is of the same family) all summer. Gray foliage means that it will not stand too much garden water.

Planting Group 3

30   Coprosma baurei 'Aurea'

Coprosma baurei 'Aurea' (*C. repens variegata*)   Zone 9

(Trailing Variegated Coprosma)

30   An excellent, rapid-growing ground cover. Best near the coast. The dark green leaves shine like a mirror and have greenish-yellow blotches. Grows to about 3 ft.   Planting Group 1

31   Coprosma kirkii

Coprosma kirkii   Zone 9

31   A low-growing, spreading, small-leaf variety of the Mirror Plant, used as a ground cover or as a very low shrub. Excellent bank cover, especially near the coast.

Planting Group 1

Correa pulchella Zone 9

(Australian Fuchsia)

32 An excellent, low-growing, compact shrub to 2 ft that is covered from mid-winter through spring with dainty, pink, tubular flowers about 1 in. long. Grows in the sun and, like so many of the plants from Australia, it requires excellent drainage and only small amounts of water. Planting Group 3

32 *Correa pulchella*

33 *Cotoneaster dammeri*

Cotoneaster dammeri Zone 7

(Bearberry Cotoneaster)

33 Grows only 6 in. high and forms a dense mat that will hang straight down over a wall. Bright green foliage about 1 in. long. White flowers, red berries. Planting Group 1

35 *Cotoneaster horizontalis*

Cotoneaster horizontalis Zone 4

(Rock Cotoneaster)

35 Flat, spreading shrub that loses its foliage in the winter but it is never missed because the plant is so heavily covered with bright-red berries. Good in sun or shade. Very effective as a low divider to stop traffic or as a mass ground cover. Planting Group 1

34 *Cotoneaster glaucophyllus*

Cotoneaster glaucophyllus Zone 5

(Gray Leafed Cotoneaster)

34 Low, bushy plant with small, gray-green foliage and bright-red berries. Excellent low-growing shrub for a dry area. Planting Group 2

Cotoneaster microphyllus Zone 4

(Rockspray Cotoneaster)

36 A low-growing, 1 ft evergreen with tiny foliage and rose-red berries that hold all winter. Excellent bank cover. Planting Group 1

36 *Cotoneaster microphyllus*

37   Cyperus alternifolius

39   Daphne cneorum

Cyperus alternifolius   Zone 9

37   Reed-like stems headed with fine, feathery foliage resembling a
Palm. Thrives best in a moist spot. Will grow in shallow water such as a
fish pond. Sun or shade.   Planting Group 1

Daphne burkwoodii 'Somerset'   Zone 4

38   Evergreen to about 0°, then semi-evergreen in the colder areas.
Erect, compact growth to about 4 ft with closely set, narrow leaves and
small clusters of fragrant, pink flowers. Needs excellent drainage, even
a raised bed.   Planting Group 2

38   Daphne burkwoodii 'Somerset'

Daphne cneorum   Zone 6

(Garland Daphne)

39   Low evergreen, growing 9–12 in. and spreading 2–3 ft. Small,
gray-green foliage 1 in. long and covered with fragrant, pink flowers in
April or May. Recommended for the Northwest, but not too good in
California, where it must be top dressed with peat and loam after
bloom to prevent dieback.   Planting Group 1

40   Daphne odora 'Marginata'

Daphne odora 'Marginata'   Zone 8

(Winter Daphne)

40   A superior, dense, low shrub with gold-margined leaves and
small clusters of intensely fragrant, pink and white flowers. Temper-
mental around San Francisco, but blooms well elsewhere. Full sun in
the cooler areas, but shade where it is warm. Blooms January to March.
Needs excellent drainage and should be planted higher or on a slight
mound to prevent "collar rot."   Planting Group 5

Deutzia gracilis   Zone 6

41   Deciduous. Graceful, 2–4 ft shrub with an abundance of pure-
white flowers in the spring.   Planting Group 1

41   Deutzia gracilis

44   *Equisetum hyemale*

43   *Diosma pulchrum*

Diosma pulchrum (Coleonema pulchrum)   Zone 9
(Pink Breath of Heaven)

43   A dwarf, compact, bushy shrub with heather-like foliage, and masses of tiny pink flowers during spring and summer. Should be pruned heavily after blooming. Sun.   Planting Group 1

Diosma ericoides (Coleonema album)   Zone 9
(Breath of Heaven or Baby's Breath)

42   Taller growing than the pink variety, with arching branches. Excellent landscape shrub to lighten the effect of a heavy, solid shrubbery line. Masses of small, white flowers. Should be kept pruned to 3 ft.   Planting Group 1

Equisetum hyemale   Zone 9
(Horsetail Reed Grass)

44   A rush-like, deep green, tropical grass with jointed stems. Excellent for tropical effect but should be contained. Requires abundant water; even grows in a shallow fish pond.   Planting Group 1

42   *Diosma ericoides*

Erica carnea 'Springwood Pink' and 'Springwood White'
Zone 5

45–46   Delightful, early, spring-blooming shrubs to about 1 ft tall. Sometimes used as a bank ground cover. There are many varieties used and grown mostly in the Northwest but are available sometimes in Northern California. The plants need excellent drainage and never should be allowed to dry out.   Planting Group 2

45   *Erica carnea* 'Springwood Pink'

46   Erica carnea 'Springwood White'

47   Eriogonum arborescens

Eriogonum arborescens   Zone 9

(Santa Cruz Island Buckwheat)

47   Narrow, gray foliage on a bush that grows 2–4 ft across. Flowers are pink, in long, flat clusters that may be dried for flower arrangements. Stands winds and fog, but must have good drainage. Not too good inland.   Planting Group 3

Euryops pectinatus   Zone 9

48   An evergreen perennial that blooms almost the year around. Yellow daisy flowers and gray-green foliage. Drought resistant and thrives even in ocean winds.   Planting Group 1

48   Euryops pectinatus

50   Gardenia jasminoides 'Mystery'

49   Festuca glauca

Festuca glauca   Zone 8

(Blue Fescue)

49   Hardly a shrub, but an attractive, ornamental, blue grass, which grows in small clumps to 6 in. Excellent, small plant for borders or edging. Widely used for "Oriental" garden effects.   Planting Group 2

FERNS
All Ferns are listed together in the Medium-Growing Shrubs section, regardless of height.

Gardenia jasminoides 'Mystery'   Zone 8

(Cape Jasmine)

50   A handsome 3–4 ft shrub with large, fragrant, white flowers, ideal for corsages. Should be planted in soil composed of sand, peat, and leaf mold. Must have perfect drainage. Should not be cultivated. Feed regularly with blood meal, and, if leaves are still yellow, try iron sequestrene. Best where there is heat. Do not plant in full shade.

Planting Group 2

Gardenia jasminoides 'Veitchii'   Zone 8

52   Smaller flowers than *G. j.* 'Mystery', but blooms more profusely and over a longer period. Needs feeding regularly and, if leaves turn yellow, add iron and mulch with leaf mold and peat. Best in the warmer valleys. Requires excellent drainage.   Planting Group 2

51   Gardenia jasminoides 'Radicans'

52   *Gardenia jasminoides 'Veitchii'*

Gardenia jasminoides 'Radicans'   Zone 8

51   A low form of Gardenia that grows only a foot tall. Has miniature flowers about the size of a silver dollar. A beautiful little rock plant, but, like the other two Gardenia varieties described, difficult to raise. For most people, it will either grow nicely or not at all. If you like Gardenias, it is worthwhile trying. Requires good drainage.   Planting Group 2

53   *Gaultheria procumbens*

54   Gaultheria shallon

Gaultheria procumbens   Zone 3
(Wintergreen)

53   Excellent ground cover with a creeping habit forming a mat of dark, fragrant, waxy green foliage which turns bronze in the fall. White flowers in the spring and large, red berries in the fall. Needs very well-drained soil.   Planting Group 1

Gaultheria shallon   Zone 5
(Salal or Lemon Leaf)

54   Native to coastal areas from mid-California to British Columbia. The cut branches are collected in the wild and sold by florists as "lemon leaves." Will grow in poor soil and with neglect to about 2 ft but in good garden conditions, in the shade, to over 4 ft. White or pinkish flowers in clusters in the spring and edible, black fruit in the fall.   Planting Group 1

Grevillea 'Noell'   Zone 9

55 . A clean, low, compact plant with needle-like, bright green foliage and rose-red blooms in the spring. Excellent bank cover.   Planting Group 1

55   Grevillea 'Noell'

56 Hebe buxifolia

58 Hebe 'Evansi'

Hebe 'Evansi' (*H. rubra*)   Zone 9

58   The leaves are a blend of dark green and reddish-purple, about 2 in. long. Flowers are 3 in. and reddish-purple. Blooms in summer.
                                 Planting Group 1

60 Hebe menziesii

Hebe buxifolia   Zone 9

56   Low, compact shrub with small, ½ in. long leaves, and small, white flowers. Very useful for low edging or a globe-shaped plant. All *Hebes* stand heavy pruning.   Planting Group 1

57 Hebe 'Co-ed'

Hebe 'Co-ed'   Zone 8

57   One of the newer varieties and one of the best. A compact bush with rich, dark green leaves and purplish-pink flowers borne in profusion during spring and summer. Like all *Hebes* does better in coastal areas than the hot interior.   Planting Group 1

59 Hebe imperialis

Hebe imperialis   Zone 8

59   Compact, rounded shrub to 4 ft. Clean, glossy-green foliage, 1–3 in. long and reddish-purple flower spikes. Good coastal plant. Stands heavy pruning.   Planting Group 1

Hebe menziesii   Zone 9

60   A small, shiny-leafed, compact plant with arching branches and a profusion of small, showy, white flowers. Best in the cool, coastal areas and in the shade.   Planting Group 4

61 *Hebe 'Patty's Purple'*

62 *Helleborus lividus corsicus*

Hebe 'Patty's Purple'   Zone 8

61 A small variety usually not more than 18 in. tall. Very nice for compact borders. Purple flowers in spring and summer.

Planting Group 1

Helleborus lividus corsicus   Zone 8
(Corsican Hellebore)

62 Excellent perennial to 2 ft with blue-green leaves with sharply toothed edges. Clusters of large, chartreuse flowers. Flowers in late fall and winter in Southern California but in the Northwest they arrive in March and April. Best in partial shade.   Planting Group 4

Hypericum calycinum   Zone 5
(Aaron's Beard)

63 Excellent ground cover to 1 ft in height. Bright yellow flowers in the spring or summer, either in full sun or partial shade. Spreads by underground runners and once established will grow without too much water. It can be hard to control in a garden.   Planting Group 1

63 *Hypericum calycinum*

Hypericum moseranum   Zone 8
(Gold Flower)

64 A delightful, low, foundation plant with arching branches to 3 ft in height. Golden yellow flowers in spring and summer. Stands full sun or partial shade on the coast, but does best in partial shade in the interior.   Planting Group 1

64 *Hypericum moseranum*

Hypericum patulum henryi (H. beanii)   Zone 7
(St. John's Wort)

65 A nice, evergreen shrub to 4 ft tall, with continuous yellow blooms all summer. Stands pruning. Grows in any soil, sun or partial shade. Seldom looks like much in a container at the nursery, but develops into a wonderful plant in the garden.   Planting Group 1

65 *Hypericum patulum henryi*

66   *Ilex cornuta 'Rotunda'*

67   *Ilex crenata 'Green Island'*

Ilex cornuta 'Rotunda'   Zone 6
(Dwarf Chinese Holly)

66   Compact, low-growing Holly with dense habit of growth. Ideal for both sun or shade. Does not produce berries but is a valuable landscape plant for its excellent habits and abundance of attractive, shapely leaves.   Planting Group 1

Ilex crenata 'Green Island'   Zone 6

67   An excellent, low-growing, small-leaved plant that is so dense it looks very much like a Boxwood and can be used the same way. Usually grows to 24 in. in a nice, tight mound but can be trimmed as a hedge. Sun or part shade and usually found in the Northwest.
                                             Planting Group 1

Jasminum magnificum (J. nitidum)   Zone 10
(Angel Wing Jasmine)

68   A small, evergreen, semi-vining, spreading shrub. Large, shiny green leaves and glistening, fragrant, white flowers.
                                             Planting Group 1

68   *Jasminum magnificum*

69   *Lantana sellowiana*

Lantana sellowiana (L. montevidensis)   Zone 9
(Trailing Lantana)

69   Lavender flowers on a low, fast-spreading plant, seldom more than 1 ft, unless it can climb. Likes heat and dry soils.
                                             Planting Group 2

70   *Lavandula vera*

Lavandula vera (L. angustifolia)   Zone 7
(English Lavender)

70   Attractive, gray-green, compact shrub with fragrant, lavender spikes of flowers in the spring.   Planting Group 3

Leucothoe catesbaei 'Rainbow'   Zone 5
(Leucothoe fontanesiana)

(Drooping Leucothoe)

72   Evergreen shrub to about 3 or 4 ft. Is related to the *Andromeda* family. The leathery leaves have a bronze tint in the winter and clusters of white flowers. Does best in woodland gardens with deep soil.
                                                        Planting Group 1

72   *Leucothoe catesbaei* 'Rainbow'

71   *Leptospermum scoparium* 'Snow White'

Leptospermum scoparium 'Snow White'   Zone 9

71   A spreading, compact plant to about 4 ft with needle-like foliage and medium-sized, double white flowers with greenish centers. Flowers all spring, usually starting in December.   Planting Group 3

73   *Liriope muscari*

Loropetalum chinense   Zone 4

74   Usually this plant is a 3–4 ft shrub but sometimes taller. Neat, compact habit with drooping branches. Flowers are white to greenish-white in clusters at the end of branches. Heavy bloom in March and April with some blooms all summer. Full sun in cooler areas to partial shade inland. Needs well-drained soil with ample water.
                                                        Planting Group 4

Liriope muscari   Zone 6

73   Dark green, grass-like leaves form clumps to 12–18 in. and produce spikes of lavender flowers. Best in partial shade.
                                                        Planting Group 4

74   *Loropetalum chinense*

Mahonia aquifolium 'Compacta'   Zone 5

(Dwarf Oregon Grape)

75   The same handsome evergreen foliage and the same rich yellow clusters of flowers as the regular Oregon Grape, except it only is one-third the size, usually not more than 2 ft.   Planting Group 4

75   *Mahonia aquifolium* 'Compacta'

76 Mahonia nervosa

Mahonia nervosa   Zone 5
(Longleaf Mahonia)

76 Native from Northern California to British Columbia. A low-growing species with long, slender leaves. Full sun or deep shade. Yellow flowers in the spring. Usually 2–3 ft but will grow to 6 ft in excellent soil.   Planting Group 1

77 Moraea iridioides

Moraea iridioides (Dietes iridioides)   Zone 8
(Butterfly Iris)

77 Narrow, Iris-like foliage with stalks of white, Iris-like flowers having yellow and blue markings, bloom only when the sun shines. The flowers close up at night.   Planting Group 1

78 Myrtus communis 'Compacta'

Myrtus communis 'Compacta'   Zone 8
(Compact Myrtle)

78 Small leaves densely massed on this compact shrub. Excellent for low hedges, either trimmed or untrimmed. Fragrant foliage.
                                                       Planting Group 1

79 Myrtus ugni

Myrtus ugni (Ugni molinae)   Zone 8
(Chilean Guava)

79 Attractive, bushy shrub for partial shade in the valley, full sun on the coast. Rounded foliage less than 1 in. long. Small, white flowers in the spring and edible, reddish fruits in the fall. Likes slightly acid soil and should not be allowed to dry out. Never a good-looking plant when young in a container, but well worthwhile when older. The edible fruit is delightful.   Planting Group 1

80 Nandina domestica 'Nana Compacta'

81   Pachysandra terminalis

82   Pernettya mucronata

Pernettya mucronata   Zone 7

82   Compact evergreen shrub to about 3 ft with small, glossy, dark green foliage. Small, pinkish, bell-shaped flowers in the spring followed by very colorful berries. Each plant a different color berry: red, pink, white, or purple. Grow in acid, peaty soil with ample water. Sun in cooler areas and part shade in warmer areas.

Planting Group 5

Nandina domestica 'Nana Compacta'   Zone 6

80   More compact than *Nandina domestica.* Usually not more than 18 in. Same fine, green, lacy foliage but somewhat heavier than the regular *Nandina* and turns a spectacular red in the fall, especially in areas with lots of warm weather.   Planting Group 1

PALMS
All Palms are listed together in the Tall-Growing Shrubs section.

83   Pittosporum tobira 'Wheelerii'

Pachysandra terminalis   Zone 5

(Japanese Spurge)

81   A low-growing, 6 in., bright, glossy green, creeping plant, spreading by underground runners. Give it a rich soil on the acid side with plenty of moisture. Best in shade as it tends to yellow in the sun. Stands light traffic.   Planting Group 4

Pittosporum tobira 'Wheelerii'   Zone 8

(Wheeler's Dwarf)

83   Excellent, low-growing mound shrub with the same shiny green foliage of *Pittosporum tobira.* Requires very little maintenance. Use as a low mound or a low round hedge. Seldom more than 2 ft tall.

Planting Group 1

Polygala dalmaisiana   Zone 9

(Sweet Pea Shrub)

84   Small, evergreen, ever-blooming shrub to 3 ft. Small, gray-green leaves and quantities of pea-shaped, orchid flowers. Good drainage required. Needs full sun.   Planting Group 2

85   Potentilla fruticosa var. 'Katherine Dykes'

Potentilla fruticosa var. 'Katherine Dykes'   Zone 3

85   Low, mounding shrub with lemon-yellow flowers borne in profusion all summer. Attractive gray-green foliage. It is deciduous and will grow in poor soil, in heat, and with little water. Many other varieties available, from bright yellow to white.   Planting Group 1

87   Prunus laurocerasus 'Otto Luyken'

89   Punica granatum 'Nana'

Prunus glandulosa   Zone 4

(Dwarf Flowering Almond)

86   Deciduous, small, upright, heavily-branched shrub to about 4 ft. Varieties available are double pink and double white, blooming in January or February. Needs heavy pruning each year and can be pruned while in flower, or shortly after.   Planting Group 1

86   Prunus glandulosa

Prunus laurocerasus 'Otto Luyken'   Zone 8

87   A compact, low-growing, wide-spreading, very hardy Laurel with dark green, glossy foliage. White flower spikes on the branches in the spring.   Planting Group 1

88   Prunus laurocerasus 'Zabeliana'

Prunus laurocerasus 'Zabeliana'   Zone 7

(Zabel Laurel)

88   A valuable, spreading, evergreen shrub. The leaves are smaller and more pointed than English Laurel. Will grow to 5 or 6 ft, but can easily be kept under 3 ft by removing branches that grow up. The color is a good, bright green and the plant is very tolerant of different types of soil and sun and shade conditions.   Planting Group 1

Punica granatum 'Nana'   Zone 8

(Dwarf Pomegranate)

89   A dwarf, compact, bushy shrub. Produces single, vivid orange-red flowers in abundance. It is deciduous and of ornamental value only. Likes sun and heat.   Planting Group 1

Pyracantha 'Santa Cruz'   Zone 8

90   Excellent as a ground or a bank cover with low growth and a spreading habit. The foliage is dense and the berries are large and dark red, borne in huge clusters.   Planting Group 1

91   *Raphiolepis indica* 'Ballerina'

90   *Pyracantha* 'Santa Cruz'

Raphiolepis indica 'Ballerina'   Zone 8

91   One of the more compact varieties of this wonderful group. Seldom more than 2 ft high and about 5 ft across. The flowers are a deeper shade of pink than most of the varieties available in the trade.
                          Planting Group 1

93   *Raphiolepis indica* 'Enchantress'

Raphiolepis indica 'Clara'   Zone 8

92   This white-flowered form is a compact 3–4 ft plant. Like the rest of the *Raphiolepis,* this is a full sun plant but will take a good amount of shade.   Planting Group 1

92   *Raphiolepis indica* 'Clara'

Raphiolepis indica 'Enchantress'   Zone 8

93   Another excellent plant that is easily kept under 2 ft. Pink flowers in profusion and a very compact plant. Flowers the same as 'Springtime.'   Planting Group 1

Raphiolepis indica 'Pink Lady'   Zone 8

94   One of the most popular varieties of all. This handsome shrub grows to about 4 ft, either in full sun or in part shade. Similar to 'Springtime' in foliage and color of flowers.   Planting Group 1

94   *Raphiolepis indica* 'Pink Lady'

95   *Raphiolepis indica* 'Rosea'

96   *Raphiolepis indica* 'Springtime'

97   *Rhynchospermum jasminoides*

Raphiolepis indica 'Rosea'   Zone 8
(Pink India Hawthorn)

95   A neat, low-growing, evergreen shrub with bright, shiny green foliage. Soft pink flowers cover the bush in the spring and then bloom to a lesser degree all summer. Blue berries, in clusters in fall and winter. Will sometimes grow taller than 4 ft, but will stand pruning and should be kept under that height.   Planting Group 1

Raphiolepis indica 'Springtime'   Zone 8

96   This very attractive shrub is a beauty from February to May with a profusion of pink blooms. Like the other *Raphiolepis*, the shrub has glossy, leathery leaves and will stand heavy pruning. Full sun or part shade.   Planting Group 1

Rhynchospermum jasminoides   Zone 9
(Trachelospermum jasminoides)
(Star Jasmine)

97   Although this is a vine, we are listing it here because it is often sold as a shrub to be grown into a low mound or ground cover. It is one of our finest evergreen vines. Does equally well in sun or shade. The flowers from May to July are very fragrant, especially in the evening. Also used as a ground cover, but it is not for dry banks as it must have water and a moist location.   Planting Group 1

Many varieties of *Raphiolepis* are grown, all slightly different. To list a few: 'Apple Blossom', 'Bill Evans', 'Coates Crimson', 'Flamingo', 'Jack Evans', 'Pink Cloud', and 'Pinkie'.

98   *Ribes speciosum*

Ribes speciosum   Zone 9
(Fuchsia Flowering Gooseberry)

98   Native shrub along the coast from Baja California to San Francisco. Erect growing to 3 or 4 ft with spiny stems on thick, green leaves and deep crimson, Fuchsia-like flowers with long stamens. Likes partial shade and is an excellent barrier.   Planting Group 3

Ribes viburnifolium   Zone 8

(Evergreen Currant)

99   A California native evergreen shrub with a habit of growth that calls for ground cover use. It is spreading, half-trailing, and roots where it touches ground. The flowers are light pink to rose from February to April. Sun or partial shade on the coast, part shade inland.   Planting Group 1

100   *Rosmarinus officinalis*

Rosmarinus officinalis   Zone 7

(Rosemary)

100   Used since ancient times for cooking. Small, narrow, dark, gray-green, aromatic foliage and light blue flowers. This plant requires full sun, poor soil, and almost no water at all.   Planting Group 2

99   *Ribes viburnifolium*

102   *Sarcococca hookerana humilis*

Sarcococca hookerana humilis   Zone 7

102   Growth very low and spreading from underground roots. The flowers are very small, white, and fragrant. One of the best for low planter boxes in complete shade or partial shade. Likes a loose, leaf mold soil and acid food.   Planting Group 4

101   *Rosmarinus officinalis* 'Prostrata'

Rosmarinus officinalis 'Prostrata'   Zone 6

(Trailing Rosemary)

101   A dwarf shrub about 6–12 in. tall with deep grayish-green, fragrant foliage. The clusters of flowers are light blue. This plant enjoys poor soil and lack of water. A very dry bank is ideal, however, it is not recommended for people with hay fever, asthma, or an allergy to bees.   Planting Group 2

Saxifraga rubicunda (Bergenia cordifolia)   Zone 8

(Saxifrage)

103   A compact, perennial, evergreen plant with large, round, dark green leaves and clusters of pink flowers in early spring. Recommended for planter boxes in front of stores where the going is tough. A "tropical effect" ground cover. Likes some shade.   Planting Group 1

103   *Saxifraga rubicunda*

104   *Senecio greyi*

106   *Sollya heterophylla*

Senecio greyi   Zone 7

104   One of the most handsome gray plants, and, like almost all gray plants, needs only minimum amounts of water and a well-drained soil. Grows to 3, sometimes 4, ft in full sun. Leaves leathery, gray-green with silver edge.   Planting Group 3

Sollya heterophylla   Zone 9

(Australian Bluebell Creeper)

106   Evergreen, half shrub, half vine with masses of brilliant blue, ½ in. bells throughout most of the summer. Full sun or part shade on the coast, part shade inland. Very satisfactory ground cover.
                                                    Planting Group 3

105   *Skimmia japonica* (Female)

Skimmia japonica (Female)   Zone 5

105   Slow-growing, low, shade plant. In California, it needs special attention to soil condition. Use peat, leaf mold, and sand. Grows where Azaleas grow. Male plants are needed for pollination and grow taller. Female plants produce clusters of Holly-like, bright red berries. Best in mass planting.   Planting Group 4

105   *Skimmia japonica* (Male)

Skimmia japonica (Male)   Zone 5

105A   This plant grows taller than the female and is needed for pollination. The heavy spring bloom makes this a desirable plant even without the females close by. *Skimmia* should not be allowed to dry out during the summer.   Planting Group 4

107   Strelitzia reginae

108   Teucrium chamaedrys

Strelitzia reginae   Zone 9

(Bird of Paradise)

107   Exotic, orange, blue, and white "birds" on stiff stems. Plants do best in rich, well-drained soil and react favorably to acid food. Full sun on the coast, part shade inland.   Planting Group 1

Teucrium chamaedrys   Zone 7

(Dwarf Germander)

108   Low, evergreen shrub with glossy leaves and reddish-purple flowers. Plant in full sun in a well-drained soil. It thrives in a hot, dry location and will rot in a heavy, wet soil.   Planting Group 3

109   Viburnum davidii

Viburnum davidii   Zone 7

109   This low-growing evergreen has deeply-creased, large leaves that densely cover the plant. Clusters of white flowers in June followed with light blue berries. Best in the Northwest or in the cooler parts of Northern California.   Planting Group 5

Westringia rosmariniformis   Zone 9

(Australian Rosemary)

110   An Australian shrub, also known as Victorian Rosemary. Wind tolerant and drought resistant. Rosemary-like leaves light gray-green in color, and small white flowers in the spring borne in profusion (all year in the milder climates). Needs a light, well-drained soil in the sun.   Planting Group 3

110   Westringia rosmariniformis

MEDIUM-GROWING SHRUBS

Plants described in this group usually grow from 4–8 ft or usually are kept pruned to this height. All plants evergreen unless otherwise mentioned.

Abelia 'Edward Goucher' Zone 6

(Pink Abelia)

111 Graceful, arching branches of bronzy foliage, laden with lavender-pink, bell-shaped flowers throughout the summer. Sun or shade. Planting Group 1

111 *Abelia* 'Edward Goucher'

Abelia grandiflora Zone 6

(Glossy Abelia)

112 Graceful evergreen shrub with fragrant, white, bell-shaped flowers in spring and summer. The rich, dark green foliage turns to bronze and then to red as soon as the cold weather comes. An old standby in land-scaping. Planting Group 1

112 *Abelia grandiflora*

Abutilon hybridum Zone 9

(Flowering Maple)

113 Medium-sized, upright shrub with arching branches holding bell-like flowers. Various colors: red, yellow, white, etc. Very attractive to hummingbirds. Planting Group 4

113 *Abutilon hybridum*

116   Aralia sieboldii

Aralia sieboldii (Fatsia japonica)   Zone 9

(Glossy Aralia)

116   Excellent for tropical effects in shade; however, it will take all but
the hottest sun. In the sun it loses its luster and becomes yellowish.
Makes a wonderful tub plant when planted in clumps of three or
four.   Planting Group 1, best in 5

114   Althaea syriaca

Althaea syriaca (Hibiscus syriacus)

(Rose of Sharon)   Zone 5

114   Deciduous. Grown extensively in the
colder climates, it is hardy to zero but loves the
warm climate of the interior. Wide color range:
red, rose, purple, blue, and white, both single
and double flowers.   Planting Group 1

Arbutus unedo 'Compacta'   Zone 7

(Compact Strawberry Tree)

117   A much more compact form of *Arbutus
unedo*. Foliage somewhat smaller. Very colorful
and attractive. Deer proof.   Planting Group 1

117   Arbutus unedo 'Compacta'

115   Aralia elegantissima

Aralia elegantissima   Zone 10
(Dizygotheca elegantissima)

(False Aralia)

115   An unexcelled evergreen shrub with
deep green, heavily-serrated leaves. If given
good light when young it turns a deep bronze-
purple with smaller leaves. Ideal indoor plant
in a bright area.   Planting Group 2

118   Aucuba japonica

Aucuba japonica   Zone 7

(Dwarf Aucuba)

118   Bright red berries on this tropical-appearing 4–5 ft plant. The foliage is shiny dark green and, like the rest of the *Aucubas*, it is an excellent plant for a shady area. It needs a male plant nearby to pollenize it for berry production.   Planting Group 4

121   Aucuba japonica 'Variegata'

Aucuba japonica 'Variegata'   Zone 7

(Gold Dust Plant)

121   Male and female of the most widely used *Aucubas* which flourish in full or partial shade with plenty of water. The gold-specked foliage is 4–6 in. long and 2–3 in. wide. Stands heavy pruning, but usually grows only about 12–18 in. a year and to about 6 ft. Female plants produce large, red berries when planted with male varieties. Named male plants not too plentiful in most nurseries.   Planting Group 4

119   Aucuba japonica 'Crotonifolia'

Aucuba japonica 'Crotonifolia'   Zone 6

119   Another outstanding *Aucuba*. This one is a male plant with brightly colored leaves which does wonders for a shady garden when mixed with other *Aucubas* to induce berries. It likes only a little sun. Like most of the other *Aucubas*, this one grows to about 6 ft and can stand heavy pruning.   Planting Group 4

Aucuba japonica 'Picturata'   Zone 7

120   Large, bright golden leaves with a green edge. Very showy. Like the rest of the *Aucubas* this one likes the shade and will grow with little care. (Female.)   Planting Group 4

120   Aucuba japonica 'Picturata'

122   *Berberis darwinii*

125   *Brunfelsia calycina* 'Floribunda'

123   *Berberis julianae*

124   *Berberis thunbergii* 'Atropurpurea'

Berberis darwinii   Zone 3

(Darwin Barberry)

122   One of the showiest of the Barberries, it bears masses of small, holly-shaped, dark green leaves. Clusters of orange-yellow flowers in spring, followed by dark blue berries. It will grow higher but should be kept under 6 ft.   Planting Group 1

Berberis julianae   Zone 7

(Wintergreen Barberry)

123   Evergreen to semi-deciduous. Very leathery, spiny-toothed, 3 in. long, dark green leaves with reddish fall color. Formidable as a barrier hedge, as this is one of the thorniest. Grows to 6 ft.   Planting Group 1

Berberis thunbergii 'Atropurpurea'   Zone 3

(Red Leaf Japanese Barberry)

124   Deciduous. Leaves are reddish-purple when planted in the sun but green in the shade. Excellent low, 4–5 ft hedge, or as a mass planting with thorns where no traffic is wanted. *B. thunbergii,* the green variety, also is available.   Planting Group 1

Brunfelsia calycina 'Floribunda'   Zone 8
(*B. pauciflora* 'Floribunda')

(Yesterday, Today and Tomorrow Shrub)

125   Compact shrub grows to 5 ft in shade or part sun. The interesting common name comes from the white flowers (yesterday), bright blue, fragrant flowers (today), and blue buds (tomorrow), all showing at the same time. Best in rich, slightly acid, well-drained soil. Long blooming period.   Planting Group 4

128   *Calliandra tweedii*

127   *Calliandra inequilatera*

Calliandra inequilatera (C. haematocephala)   Zone 9

(Pink Powder Puff)

127   Medium-sized, tropical, evergreen shrub. Lots of bright pink stamens that look like a huge powder puff which contrasts with the rich, green foliage.   Planting Group 2

Calliandra tweedii   Zone 9

(Brazilian Flame Bush)

128   Leaves are lacy and fern-like. Each branch bears medium-sized heads of fluffy, vivid scarlet stamens, shaped like pom-poms. Blooms all spring and summer.

Planting Group 2

Buxus sempervirens   Zone 5

(English Boxwood)

126   Tall growing; usually used as a trimmed pyramid, in globes, or in a hedge.

Planting Group 1

PLANTING GUIDE

Following each description is a planting group guide. Here, again, individual conditions will vary so the planting instructions are general. An attempt has been made to give you a clue to the general soil conditions needed for each plant. You should check local conditions with your nursery.

Group 1 means the plant will grow in the sun without special treatment unless otherwise mentioned.

Group 2 means the plant will grow in the sun but must have excellent drainage.

Group 3 means the plant will grow in the sun but must have excellent drainage and only minimum amounts of water; usually gray foliage plants.

Group 4 means the plant will grow in the shade without special treatment.

Group 5 means the plant will grow in the shade but must have excellent drainage and special soil mixture.

TEMPERATURE RATINGS

Zone 10	40° to 30°
Zone 9	30° to 20°
Zone 8	20° to 10°
Zone 7	10° to 0°
Zone 6	0° to −10°
Zone 5	−10° to −20°
Zone 4	−20° to −30°
Zone 3	−30° to −40°

Temperatures suggested in this book are approximate. The growing conditions, for example, a warm, late fall, often will keep the plants from hardening off and a sudden cold snap has been known to freeze plants 20° above the normal freezing point.

126   *Buxus sempervirens*

CAMELLIAS

Truly the aristocrat of all garden plants. No other group of plants (except Roses) commands the attention that this lovely group does. Here, again, we are listing all Camellias in the medium group, knowing full well they will grow higher in time, however, from a landscape point of view, 6–8 ft is the height to which most varieties can be kept with a minimum of pruning.

They grow best with an eastern exposure or full shade in the hot interior, with a soil rich in humus and peat moss and in a moist and well-drained location. Avoid planting any deeper than grown in the nursery and avoid a poorly drained location. Best when heavily mulched, especially in the warmer interior. If planting in a sunny location, place the plant so the leaves shade the soil (even a slight tilt) or place a good-sized boulder or two in front to keep the sun off the ground.

129   *Camellia japonica* 'Grandiflora Rosea'

130   *Camellia japonica* 'Kumasaka'

CAMELLIA JAPONICA

'Adolphe Audusson Special'	red and white
'Alba Plena'	double white
'Bella Romana'	light pink-striped carmine
'Betty Sheffield Supreme'	white, rose border
'Blood of China'	deep salmon-red
'Carter's Sunburst'	pale pink, rose-striped
'Chandleri Elegans'	rose-pink and white
'C. M. Wilson'	light pink
'Daikagura'	bright rose-pink and white
'Debutante'	light pink
'Drama Girl'	salmon rose-pink
'E. G. Waterhouse'	formal pink
'Eleanor Hagood'	pale pink
'Elena Nobile'	flame red
'Fimbriata Alba'	white, fringed petals
'Finlandia'	white
'Finlandia Variegated' ('Margaret Jack')	white and crimson
'Francine'	rose-pink
'Glen 40'	deep red
'Grandiflora Rosea'	deep pink
'Guilio Nuccio Variegated'	coral-rose-pink and white
'Herme (Jordan's Pride)	pink, deep pink stripes with white edge
'Kramer's Supreme'	rich red
'Kumasaka'	rose-pink
'Lallarook' ('Laurel Leaf')	pink and white
'Magnoliaeflora'	blush-pink
'Mathotiana' ('Julia Drayton')	crimson
'Mathotiana Alba'	white
'Pearl Maxwell'	shell-pink
'Pink Perfection'	shell-pink
'Pope Pius IX'	cherry red
'Prof. Charles S. Sargent'	dark red
'Purity'	white
'Shiro Chan'	white

CAMELLIA SASANQUA

'Apple Blossom'	blush-pink
'Jean May'	shell-pink
'Showa No Sakae'	soft pink
'Showa Supreme'	soft pink
'Sparkling Burgundy'	ruby-rose
'Tanya'	deep rose-pink
'White Doves'	white
'Yae Arare'	white
'Yuletide'	orange-red, yellow stamens

130A   *Camellia japonica* 'Eleanor Hagood'

130C   *Camellia japonica* 'Grandiflora Rosea'

130D   *Camellia japonica* 'Villa de Nantes'

130E   *Camellia japonica* 'Finlandia Variegated'

130G   *Camellia japonica* 'Chandleri Elegans'

130H   *Camellia japonica* 'Mrs. Charles Cobb'

130I   *Camellia japonica* 'Glen 40'

130J   *Camellia japonica* 'Mrs. D.W. Davis'

130K   *Camellia japonica* 'Mathotiana Alba'

130L   *Camellia japonica* 'Kramer's Supreme'

130M   *Camellia japonica* 'Shiro Chan'

130N   *Camellia japonica* 'C.M. Wilson'

130O   *Camellia reticulata* 'Crimson Robe'

130P   *Camellia reticulata* 'Chaings Temple'

130Q   *Camellia reticulata* 'Cornelian'

130R   *Camellia sasanqua* 'Jean May'

130S   Camellia sasanqua 'Shishi-Gashira'

130T   Camellia sasanqua 'Setsugekka'

132   Cassia artemisioides

131   Carissa grandiflora

Cassia artemisioides   Zone 9

(Wormwood Senna)

132   Attractive, light-textured shrub, 3–4 ft tall. Gray foliage with
light yellow flowers during winter and spring. Like most other gray
foliage plants, it requires very good drainage.   Planting Group 3

Planting Group 3

Carissa grandiflora   Zone 9
(*C. macrocarpa*)
(Natal Plum)

131   A round shrub to about 5 or 6 ft with
glossy foliage. Often used as an attractive and
useful informal hedge. The thorns will dis-
courage traffic, and the shiny, red fruit looks
like a plum, but tastes much better.
                                Planting Group 2

Ceanothus impressus   Zone 8

(Santa Barbara Ceanothus)

133   Low growing (about 5 ft high), with spreading, small, crinkly,
dark green foliage. The deep blue flowers are quite large. One of the
best.   Planting Group 2

133   Ceanothus impressus

Ceanothus 'Julia Phelps'   Zone 8

134   Rich, cobalt-blue flowers that are fairly small but in dense
clusters. The plant is garden tolerant and grows to 6 or 7 ft in height
with a 10 ft spread. When in bloom the intense blue color is stunning.
One of the best steep-hillside plants.   Planting Group 2

Ceanothus 'Mountain Haze'   Zone 8

135   The foliage is dark green with small, soft blue flowers in April and May. One of the best garden varieties in the 4–6 ft class. Will stand pruning.   Planting Group 2

Cestrum parqui   Zone 9

(Night Blooming Jessamine)

136   Just an ordinary, green shrub by day with small, greenish-yellow flowers, but at night one of the most strikingly fragrant shrubs in the trade. Often freezes to the ground but comes back up in the spring. Best as a 5–7 ft shrub. Needs heavy cutting to keep it in hand. Does best in a warmer climate.   Planting Group 1

135   Ceanothus 'Mountain Haze'

134   Ceanothus 'Julia Phelps'

136   Cestrum parqui

Chamelaucium ciliatum (C. uncinatum)   Zone 9

(Geraldton Wax Flower)

137   Medium- to tall-growing shrub that should be kept pruned to a maximum of 6 ft. It has light green, needle-like foliage, and sprays of light pink to white flowers of a waxy appearance. The flowers last for a long time. Full sun and excellent drainage required.
                   Planting Group 3

138   Choisya ternata

Choisya ternata   Zone 8

(Mexican Orange or Mexican Mock Orange)

138   A very useful and desirable 3–5 ft shrub for sun or shade. Foliage is rich green and heavy. Fragrant flowers borne in Orange Blossom-like clusters. Will turn yellow immediately if drainage is poor.
                   Planting Group 2

137   Chamelaucium ciliatum

141   *Citrus* 'Tangerine'

142   *Citrus* 'Meyer Lemon'

Citrus 'Meyer Lemon' (*C.* 'Improved Meyer')   Zone 9
(Dwarf Meyer Lemon)

142   One of the best dual-purpose plants in the trade today. Dwarf in habit. Good, bold green foliage; constantly covered with fragrant white flowers; plenty of ripe fruit most of the year. Requires good drainage, regular fertilization, and full sun. Water sparingly, but deeply.   Planting Group 2

139   *Citrus* 'Kumquat'

140   *Citrus* 'Grapefruit'

143   *Coprosma baueri*

Citrus   Zone 9

139–141   Many varieties are available and, if you are fortunate enough to live in a warm area, try one near the front door, especially one grown on dwarf understock. Bright, shiny leaves, fragrant flowers, and attractive fruit. Only a few of the many varieties are pictured.
                                                                    Planting Group 3

144   *Cordyline stricta*

145   *Corokia cotoneaster*

Coprosma baueri (C. repens)   Zone 9

(Mirror Plant)

143   Excellent shrub in the coastal area. Leaves are round, shiny and green. Will grow taller than 6 ft, but it should be pruned to below that height. In coastal areas, it will grow in full sun, shade inland. One of the few plants that will grow (and look good) under that "unsightly deck."   Planting Group 1

146   *Corylus avellana* 'Contorta'

Cordyline stricta   Zone 9

(Palm Lily)

144   A fine container plant, indoors or outdoors. Excellent tropical-effect plant in a sunny location near the coast or in the shade in the desert. This plant will grow to 10 ft, but may be kept narrow and much smaller.   Planting Group 3

Corylus avellana 'Contorta'   Zone 4

(Walking Stick)

146   Branches on this twisted Filbert make a very unusual display. A fantastic container plant that will grow to 7 or 8 ft but best when kept around 4 ft.   Planting Group 1

Corokia cotoneaster   Zone 8

145   Slow growing to 7 or 8 ft, but usually kept in the 4 ft range. Delightful branch pattern made up of almost black, thin, contorted branches. Very dark, ¾-in. leaves that are dusty white underneath; hundreds of tiny, bright yellow flowers in the spring. Excellent tub plant that tolerates sun or part shade but needs fast-draining, alkaline soil.   Planting Group 2

Crassula argentea (C. ovata)   Zone 9

(Jade Plant)

147   Excellent house plant or outdoor container plant as well as an excellent landscape plant in a mild climate. This succulent has fleshy leaf pads, 1–2 in. long, and lovely, pink flowers in early spring.
Planting Group 1

147   *Crassula argentea*

148   *Crataegus contorta*

Crotalaria agatiflora   Zone 8

(Canary Bird Bush)

149   The flowers are chartreuse. A great favorite among flower arrangers. The foliage is gray-green and the 1½ in. flowers are in clusters for a foot or more along the stem. Grows in full sun and should be pruned and thinned regularly.   Planting Group 2

Crataegus contorta   Zone 5

(Snake Hawthorn)

148   A unique, twisted form of *Crataegus* that makes an excellent bonsai both in a pot or in the garden. Small, double red flowers. Usually found in the Northwest.   Planting Group 1

Cydonia japonica (Chaenomeles japonica)   Zone 5

(Flowering Quince)

150   Deciduous. Winter flowering in red, white, and pink. The flowers are excellent for flower arrangement. The shrub makes a wonderful, untrimmed hedge if you have enough room. The thorns will stop all traffic. A number of varieties available in most nurseries.   Planting Group 1

149   *Crotalaria agatiflora*

Cytisus   Zone 6

(Scotch Broom)

Small- to medium-sized shrubs with tiny, bright green leaves. Flower in early spring when long sprays of blooms appear along the branches.

'Burkwoodi'

Deep red blooms, upright. Not shown.

'Hollandia'

151   Purplish-red blooms, upright.

Lydia (Genista lydia)

152   Yellow flowers, spreading, prostrate habit. Blooms late.

Kewensis

153   Creamy white flowers, dwarf, spreading.

'Moonbeam'

154   Glowing moonbeam yellow.

'Peter Pan'

Red blooms, dwarf growing. Not shown.

Praecox

155   Creamy yellow flowers on arching branches.

'St. Mary's'

Snow-white blooms, upright growth. Not shown.

150   *Cydonia japonica*

Cytisus lydia

151 *Cytisus* 'Hollandia'

153 *Cytisus kewensis*

154 *Cytisus* 'Moonbeam'

155 *Cytisus praecox*

156   Daubentonia tripetii

158   Erica melanthera 'Rosea'

Daubentonia tripetii (Sesbania tripetii)   Zone 8

(Scarlet Wisteria Tree)

156   Deciduous. A fast-growing shrub to 7 or 8 ft with wide, lacy leaves. Showy, burnt orange clusters of pea-shaped flowers reminiscent of Wisteria. Contrary to its common name, it is not a tree or a Wisteria or scarlet. Short-lived.   Planting Group 1

Erica melanthera 'Rosea' (E. canaliculata 'Rosea')   Zone 9

(Pink Scotch Heather)

158   A tall shrub with long plumes of pink flowers during the winter. Should be pruned for the flowers during, or right after, flowering to a 4–5 ft height, but will grow higher. Grows in sun or partial shade. Requires a very well-drained, peat or sandy acid soil.
          Planting Group 2

157   Echium fastuosum

Echium fastuosum   Zone 9

(Pride of Madeira)

157   Large, 4–5 ft clumps of gray-green, narrow leaves on a rounded mound. Large, Delphinium-like spikes of blue-purple flowers (up to 3 ft above the plant) give a bold effect. Good at the seashore or dry location and enjoys poor soil.   Planting Group 2

Erica melanthera 'Rubra'   Zone 9
(E. canaliculata 'Rubra')

(Red Scotch Heather)

159   A compact shrub of medium height with dark green, needle-like foliage. The flowers come on the new wood in long plumes of deep pink in the late fall. The shrub should be cut back to encourage new growth after blooming. Requires a peat loam soil on the acid side and very good drainage.   Planting Group 2

159   Erica melanthera 'Rubra'

161　*Eugenia myrtifolia* 'Compacta'

160　*Escallonia rubra*

162　*Euonymus alata*

Escallonia rubra　　　　　Zone 8
(Red Escallonia)

160　A medium-sized bush 5–6 ft high, which will grow in sun or shade and stand any amount of pruning. Flowers are red in nice clusters with shiny, glossy green background foliage. Stands seashore conditions.　　　Planting Group 1

Eugenia myrtifolia 'Compacta'　　Zone 9
(*Syzygium paniculatum* 'Compacta')

161　Dwarf form of *E. myrtifolia* on which the new foliage stays red for a longer period of time. With little effort it can be kept at any point in the 3–6 ft range and can be shaped.
　　　　　　　　　　Planting Group 1

Euonymus alata　　　　　Zone 3
(Winged Burning Bush)

162　A compact, deciduous shrub that grows slowly to 5 ft and is a must in the colder areas; this one has foliage that turns the most brilliant red of any garden shrub.　Planting Group 1

163　*Euonymus japonica*

Euonymus japonica　　　　　Zone 5
(Evergreen Euonymus)

163　Good, slow-growing, compact shrub for foundation planting. Most of the *Euonymus* family are inclined to mildew in coastal areas but are excellent in the hot interior.　　　Planting Group 1

165   *Euonymus japonica* 'Aureo-variegata'

166   *Euonymus japonica* 'Silver Queen'

164   *Euonymus japonica* 'Aureo-marginata'

Euonymus japonica 'Aureo-marginata'
Zone 5

(Golden Euonymus)

164   Green leaves with golden edges.
Planting Group 1

Euonymus japonica 'Aureo-variegata'
Zone 5

(Gold Spot Euonymus)

165   On this outstanding variety, leaves are gold in the center with dark green edges.
Planting Group 1

Euonymus japonica 'Silver Queen'   Zone 5

166   Large, evergreen foliage. Metallic green leaves with creamy white margins.   Planting Group 1

TEMPERATURE RATINGS

Zone 10	40° to 30°
Zone 9	30° to 20°
Zone 8	20° to 10°
Zone 7	10° to 0°
Zone 6	0° to −10°
Zone 5	−10° to −20°
Zone 4	−20° to −30°
Zone 3	−30° to −40°

Temperatures suggested in this book are approximate. The growing conditions, for example, a warm, late fall, often will keep the plants from hardening off and a sudden cold snap has been known to freeze plants 20° above the normal freezing point.

FERNS

There is a Fern for practically any shady or partially shady spot in the garden. All require good drainage and must have a soil rich in humus. The softness they bring to the garden is worth the extra care they require. All Ferns are listed together in the Medium-Growing Shrubs section regardless of height.

167   Adiantum pedatum

168   Alsophila australis

Adiantum pedatum   Zone 4

(Five Finger Fern)

167   Native in the cooler areas along the Pacific Coast, often growing in the wild on banks where the water is dripping or excellent pot plant in a shaded garden bed.   Planting Group 5

Alsophila australis (Sphaeropteris cooperi)   Zone 9

(Australian Tree Fern)

168   A beautiful tree Fern with a slender, graceful trunk and a crown of spreading, 5–8 ft fronds. A fast grower that needs shade and regular moisture.   Planting Group 5

169   Asparagus densiflorus 'Meyers'

Asparagus densiflorus 'Myers'   Zone 9

169   Stiff, upright stems to 2 ft that are densely clothed in needle-like, deep green leaves which have a fluffy look. A very interesting plant both in the garden or as a hanging basket. (Not a True Fern.)
                          Planting Group 5

170   *Asparagus densiflorus* 'Sprengeri'

171   *Aspidium capense*

Asparagus densiflorus 'Sprengeri'   Zone 9

170   Small leaves on long, arching branches, making a mound of green foliage. Prefers shade but will grow in considerable sun on the coast. Extensively used in hanging baskets and as an indoor plant. (Not a True Fern.)   Planting Group 5

Aspidium capense   Zone 9
(Leather Leaf Fern)

171   The triangular fronds are a deep glossy green, firm textured and excellent for flower arrangements. Best in partial shade to 2 ft, but will grow in full sun in some areas.   Planting Group 5

172   *Asplenium bulbiferum*

Asplenium bulbiferum   Zone 9
(Mother Fern)

172   Exotic, long, light green fronds, which remind one of Carrot leaves. The new Fern is produced in the axil of its fronds. Prefers shade. Grows to 2 ft.   Planting Group 5

173   *Cyrtomium falcatum*

174   *Dicksonia antarctica*

175   *Nephrolepis exaltata*

176   *Pellaea rotundifolia*

Cyrtomium falcatum   Zone 8

(Holly Fern)

173   A coarse, Holly-like leaf with stiff, dark green fronds to 2 ft. Prefers shade.   Planting Group 5

Dicksonia antarctica   Zone 9

(Tasmanian Tree Fern)

174   Hardiest of the tree Ferns. Will take sun on the coast and is excellent as a tub plant. Has a dark brown trunk with a heavy crown of feathery fronds, often as many as 50. Much more compact than the other tree Ferns, so more desirable for the small garden.
                    Planting Group 5

Nephrolepis exaltata   Zone 9

(Boston Sword Fern)

175   The upright Boston Sword Fern grows in the coastal areas in Zone 9 and in many places in full sun. Vigorous grower and divides easily. Usually not more than 30 in.   Planting Group 5

Pellaea rotundifolia   Zone 9

(Round Leaf Fern)

176   Small Fern with spreading fronds to 1 ft. The leaflets are evenly spaced and about ¾ in. across. Filtered shade.   Planting Group 5

177   *Platycerium alcicorne*

Platycerium alcicorne   Zone 9

(Staghorn Fern)

177   The most common of the Staghorn group. The gray-green fronds are thick and clustered, usually to 15 or 18 in. long but sometimes to 3 ft. In nature, they grow on trees. Excellent plant for a shaded patio. Staghorn Ferns are usually grown on a slab of wood or bark, from which they often escape, and hung on a wall or tree.

Platycerium grande   Zone 9

(Staghorn Fern)

178   Very broad fronds resembling moose antlers but somewhat divided. Fertilize with blood meal or fish emulsion at the back of each clump. Excellent patio ''talking piece'' but must be protected from frosts below 27°. Do not overwater.

178   *Platycerium grande*

179   Polystichum angulare

Polystichum angulare   Zone 8
(Single Mother Fern)

179 Low-growing Fern with spreading, lacy fronds which are covered with small plantlets that reproduce readily. Excellent rock garden plant.   Planting Group 5

180   Polystichum munitum

Polystichum munitum   Zone 7
(Western Sword Fern)

180   Native to the Pacific Coast. Grows in a clump with 2 or 3 ft fronds and is best when naturalized on a woody hillside.   Planting Group 5

181   Polystichum setosum

Polystichum setosum   Zone 8
(Japanese Lace Fern)

181 Splendid, low-growing Fern with handsome, lacy, dark green foliage, usually about 1 ft tall.   Planting Group 5

Woodwardia chamissoi (W. fimbriata)   Zone 8
(Giant Chain Fern)

182 Upright growth with 4–5 ft fronds. Stands considerable sun, is excellent background plant for partially shaded areas. Gives a tropical appearance.   Planting Group 5

182   Woodwardia chamissoi

FUCHSIAS

Zone 9

There is no better place in the world to grow Fuchsias than the San Francisco Bay Area and along the California coast, 100 miles to the north or south. In most other areas, plants are available as pot plants as soon as the frosts are over. In the 40 years I have been connected with the nursery industry, I have seen more than 1,000 varieties in the trade. No attempt will be made to describe any of them. Enough to say that there are low-growing, drooping varieties; low-growing uprights; medium-growing uprights; and tall-growing uprights. They carry, in each kind, small flowers, large flowers, single flowers, and double flowers in many colors.

Planting Group 5

183   Fuchsia

183A   Fuchsia

184A   Fuchsia 'Al Stettler'

184B   Fuchsia 'Sincerely'

184C   Fuchsia 'Keepsake'

184E   Fuchsia 'Psychedelic'

184D   Fuchsia 'Happy Talk'

184F   Fuchsia

184H   Fuchsia 'Belvedere'

184G   Fuchsia

184I   Fuchsia 'Gartenmeister Bonsted'

185   *Forsythia*

187   *Genista racemosa*

186   *Garrya elliptica*

Forsythia Intermedia   Zone 4

185   Deciduous. Forsythias are grown in many varieties in other parts of the country, but on the West Coast most nurseries carry Forsythia, period, with little regard for the variety name. Will sometimes grow more than 6 ft, but normally 4–6 ft. Long sprays of bright golden flowers from January to March. A bright spot in a winter garden. Excellent for a dramatic bouquet indoors.   Planting Group 1

Garrya elliptica   Zone 9

(Coast Silk Tassel)

186   A very attractive, hardy, dense, evergreen shrub to 5 or 6 ft or more. The interesting and very attractive flowers have pendulous catkins, almost a foot long. Excellent for the seashore.
Planting Group 3

Genista racemosa (Cytisus racemosus)   Zone 8

(Sweet Broom)

187   A free-flowering shrub that will grow in any soil. The golden yellow flowers are pea-shaped and oftentimes will reseed themselves.   Planting Group 2

Gunnera chilensis   Zone 8

188   This plant is reminiscent of a giant Rhubarb. The leaves are often 5 ft or more in diameter. Needs soil rich in humus, high in nitrogen, and never let it dry out. Ideal for a bog. Leaves should be cut clear back if not killed by frost. Partial shade.   Planting Group 1

189   *Hibiscus moscheutos*

188   *Gunnera chilensis*

HIBISCUS

Hibiscus are sunny, warm-weather plants for Zone 10 and high Zone 9. However, many of us consider them "fun plants" and in May, in frost areas, buy a plant and treat it as an annual. In full sun it will bloom every day with usually a dozen blooms at a time and will last until freezing weather comes.

'Agnes Gault'	tallest, hardiest, and most popular single pink. flowers up to 6 in. in diameter.
'Brilliant' ('San Diego Red')	single bright red flowers, bright green foliage.
'Butterfly'	lemon-yellow.
'California Gold'	yellow, orange center.
'Crown of Bohemia'	double yellow with orange-red throat.
'Diamond Head'	large, double deep pink
'Hula Girl'	single rich yellow with red throat.
'Kona'	full double pink.
'Red Monarch'	medium-sized plant with a compact habit of growth; double rich crimson-red.
'Ross Estey'	large, single rose with orange edges.
'White Wings'	single white, red throat.

Hibiscus moscheutos   Zone 8

(Rose Mallow, Perennial Hibiscus)

189 Hardy perennial. Stems grow to 6 or 8 ft each year. Starts blooming in late June and continues until frost, then dies down for the winter. Flowers are the largest of all Hibiscus. Some varieties up to 12 in. Colors white, pink, or red. A hot-weather plant.   Planting Group 1

190 *Hibiscus* 'White Wings'

Hibiscus rosa-sinensis (In Variety)   Zone 9

190 Very popular shrubs but actually somewhat tender for even most of California. In colder areas, with hot summers, we recommend that they be planted as annuals in April or May for the great masses of blooms they will produce all summer. Full sun and good drainage. We list some of the most popular varieties, but there are many more in the trade. Most varieties are in the 5–7 ft class, but some will easily grow to 12 ft in warmer areas of Zone 9.   All Planting Group 1

190 *Hibiscus* 'Agnes Gault'

190A   Hibiscus 'White Wings'

190B   Hibiscus 'Brilliant' ('San Diego Red')

190C   Hibiscus 'Kona'

190D   Hibiscus 'Diamond Head'

190E   Hibiscus 'Agnes Gault'

190F   Hibiscus 'Hula Girl'

190G   Hibiscus 'Crown of Bohemia'

190H   Hibiscus 'Ross Estey'

190I   Hibiscus 'Butterfly'

TEMPERATURE RATINGS

Zone 10	40° to 30°
Zone 9	30° to 20°
Zone 8	20° to 10°
Zone 7	10° to 0°
Zone 6	0° to −10°
Zone 5	−10° to −20°
Zone 4	−20° to −30°
Zone 3	−30° to −40°

Temperatures suggested in this book are approximate. The growing conditions, for example, a warm, late fall, often will keep the plants from hardening off and a sudden cold snap has been known to freeze plants 20° above the normal freezing point.

HYDRANGEA MACROPHYLLA

Deciduous. A large growing shrub, 4–6 ft high; covered in early summer with mammoth blooms, some up to 1 ft in diameter. Best in light shade. Many people make the mistake of cutting their plants down from a 5 ft plant to 2 ft during the winter. This delays blossoming until late August. Instead, thin one-third of the plant from the base in order to develop new shoots from the ground. It then will blossom in early June. Not too many nurseries carry named varieties. Some of these are:

'Hamburg'	scarlet
'Merrit's Beauty'	carmen-red
'Revelation'	brilliant red
'Trophy'	brilliant salmon-rose
'White	white

Zone 2   Planting Group 4

191 *Hydrangea*   192 *Hydrangea*

BLUE HYDRANGEAS

There aren't any. What you have seen is the result of a chemical change caused by acid soil. Pink varieties may be changed to blue by adding iron sulfate or aluminum sulfate to the soil. To keep the pink, add lime. Whites do not change color satisfactorily.

PLANTING GUIDE

Following each description is a planting group guide. Here again, individual conditions will vary so the planting instructions are general. An attempt has been made to give you a clue to the general soil conditions needed for each plant. You should check local conditions with your nurseryman.

Group 1 means the plant will grow in the sun without special treatment, unless otherwise mentioned.

Group 2 means the plant will grow in the sun, but must have excellent drainage.

Group 3 means the plant will grow in the sun, but must have excellent drainage and only minimum amounts of water, usually gray foliage plants.

Group 4 means the plant will grow in the shade, without special treatment.

Group 5 means the plant will grow in the shade, but must have excellent drainage and special soil mixture.

193   Ilex cornuta 'Burfordii'

⊛ *195   Kerria japonica*

Ilex cornuta 'Burfordii'   Zone 7

(Burford Holly)

193   This Holly will grow in the hot interior valleys. Bears heavy crops of bright red berries. Self-pollinating. The leaves are smooth, dark green with few spines. Grows to 6 ft or more but stands any amount of pruning.   Planting Group 1

194   Kalmia latifolia

Kalmia latifolia   Zone 4

(Mountain Laurel)

194   Hardy in most all zones but does not grow too well in California. Slow growing to 4 or 5 ft in the West (10–15 ft in the East). Glossy, leathery leaves with clusters of deep pink buds and lighter, 1 in., pink flowers. Same culture as Rhododendrons.   Planting Group 5

Kerria japonica   Zone 4

195   Deciduous. Open, rounded shrub to 6 ft with heavily veined, bright green foliage and bright yellow flowers from March to May. Likes part shade in warmer areas but will take full sun in cooler coastal areas.   Planting Group 1

Lantana camara   Zone 9

196–197 A popular, rapid-growing shrub that blooms most of the year. Wide range of colors and very easy to grow. In colder areas, where it gets hot in the summer, this plant is worthwhile as a summer annual, even if it freezes.

'Christine'   cerise-pink
'Orange'   orange
'Radiation'   orange-red
'White'   white
'Yellow'   yellow

Planting Group 1

197   Lantana camara 'Radiation'

196   Lantana camara 'Yellow'

Leptospermum laevigatum 'Reevesii'   Zone 9

(Dwarf Austrailian Tea Tree)

198   Leptospermum laevigatum 'Reevesii'

198 A dwarf form of *L. laevigatum.* The leaves are a little more rounded and the shrub grows more compactly. Thrives in the same trying conditions and keeps its nice appearance even with wind, heat, and drought. Good seashore plant to 6 ft.   Planting Group 1

Leptospermum scoparium 'Helene Strybing'   Zone 9

199 Fine, needle-like foliage, with dark pink, open-faced flowers about 1 in. in diameter. Some flowers almost the year around with the heavy blooming season in the early spring. Excellent cut flower. Must be planted in a well-drained location.   Planting Group 2

199   Leptospermum scoparium 'Helene Strybing'

200   Leptospermum scoparium 'Ruby Glow'

201   Leucophyllum frutescens

202   Ligustrum japonica 'Texanum'

Leptospermum scoparium 'Ruby Glow'   Zone 9

200   Another of the hybrid *Leptospermums* that is very fine. The flowers are double red and ¾ in. in diameter. Great masses of blooms in the winter and spring in such profusion that the entire shrub turns red. Needs excellent drainage or it will die almost overnight. If it does, try a new plant in another spot. A very worthwhile, 5–6 ft plant.
Planting Group 3

203   *Ligustrum ovalifolium*

Leucophyllum frutescens   Zone 8
(Texas Sage)

201   Evergreen shrub to about 6 ft with drought-resistant silver-gray foliage. Will grow near the sea or in the hottest desert. Wants sandy, well-drained soil.   Planting Group 3

Ligustrum japonica   Zone 8
(Wax Leaf Privet)

202   The leaves are waxy, dark green, spongy, and oval in appearance. Fragrant, wax-white flowers. It also gives off allergy-producing pollen in spring. Will grow higher than 6 ft, but usually kept at 3–5 ft.
Planting Group 1

Ligustrum ovalifolium   Zone 7
(California Privet)

203   The most popular hedge plant in California. Relatively inexpensive and fast growing. Will grow taller than 6 ft, but is best when kept trimmed to 4 or 5 ft. The flowers can cause hay fever.
Planting Group 1

206 *Mahonia bealei*

204 *Lippia citriodora*

Lippia citriodora (Aloysia triphylla)   Zone 8

(Lemon Verbena)

204 A leggy, loose-growing plant to about 8 ft that is not much to look at but a joy to have. It should be placed next to a path where you can pick a leaf as you go by to rub and smell. Full sun.

Planting Group 1

Mahonia aquifolium   Zone 5

(Oregon Grape)

205 Native from British Columbia to California. Dwarf, compact shrub with glossy green, Holly-like leaflets, new growth bronzy. Showy clusters of bright yellow flowers, March to May, followed by blue berries. Grows in sun or shade. Deer proof.   Planting Group 1

205 *Mahonia aquifolium*

Mahonia bealei   Zone 6

(Leatherleaf Mahonia)

206 Flat whorls of grayish-green leaves with stiff, spiny teeth on each leaflet. Excellent for the shade. Very effective against a wall, especially if lights are used to cast shadows of the leaves. Deer proof.

Planting Group 4

Mahonia lomariifolia   Zone 8

(Chinese Holly Grape)

207 Very large, grayish pinnate leaves up to 15 in. long with each leaflet having deeply-serrated and waxy margins. The flowers are larger and brighter than the American varieties. When young, grows on a single stalk; later it branches from the base creating an artistic effect. Recommended for an "Oriental Look" in the garden. Best in half shade. Can be used indoors in a sunny location with plenty of room so you can avoid contact with prickly leaves. Usually a 4–6 ft plant, but will grow to 10 ft if not cut back.   Planting Group 2

207 *Mahonia lomariifolia*

208   Mahonia pinnata

Mahonia pinnata   Zone 7

(California Holly Grape)

208   Similar to *Mahonia aquifolium,* but the leaves are more Holly-like; has similar long, yellow flowers. Will stand more heat and drought. A very fine, decorative shrub. Sun or shade. Deer proof.

Planting Group 1

209   Melianthus major

Melianthus major   Zone 9

(Honey Bush)

209   Large, blue-gray, deeply-toothed foliage 1 ft long, reddish-brown flowers in late winter or early spring. Can grow to 6 ft in a year and eventually up to 8 or 9, and about as wide. Usually too big for the small garden. Needs hand-picking of the old, dry leaves that hang on. Stands any conditions, wet or dry; hot sun or shade.

Planting Group 1

210   Michelia fuscata

Michelia fuscata (M. figo)   Zone 9

(Banana Shrub)

210   A glossy, clean shrub that will eventually grow higher but best kept under 6 ft. The flowers are creamy white with brownish backs that lightly perfume the garden with a banana-like fragrance.

Planting Group 4

211   Murraya exotica

Murraya exotica (M. paniculata)   Zone 9

(Orange Jessamine)

211   Evergreen shrub with luxurious, deep green, small foliage and quantities of small, waxy, white flowers bearing an intense orange-blossom fragrance. Not frost hardy. Likes rich, deep soil, half (or more) shade, and regular feeding of high-nitrogen fertilizer, plus iron.

Planting Group 5

212   *Myrsine africana*

213   *Myrtus communis*

214   *Nandina domestica*

Myrsine africana   Zone 9

(African Boxwood)

212   A 4–5 ft shrub similar to Boxwood with small, rounded, dark green leaves. Good in full sun or partial shade and best when kept clipped. Somewhat subject to scale insects.   Planting Group 1

Myrtus communis   Zone 7

(Common Myrtle)

213   One of the oldest shrubs still in cultivation. It dates back to ancient Greece where it was used for Victory wreaths. Rounded shrub to 5 or 6 ft with small, pointed leaves, which are dark green, glossy, and aromatic, and an abundance of small, white, fluffy flowers.
Planting Group 1

Nandina domestica   Zone 8

(Heavenly Bamboo)

214   Not a Bamboo, but the foliage and stems give that impression. Leaves are light green, tipped with red, and turn a vivid red in the autumn. White flowers followed by bright red berries. Grows in sun or shade. One of the few outdoor shrubs that can be used indoors in planters if there is enough light. Will grow higher but should be kept thinned out to not more than 5 or 6 ft.   Planting Group 1

215   *Nerium oleander* 'Single White'

216 *Nerium oleander* 'Single Pink'

217 *Nerium* freeway divider, California

Nerium oleander   Zone 8

(Oleander)

215–216–217 A wonderful, hot-weather shrub. Blooms all summer in the interior valleys, not too well on the coast. Lots of colors: white, rose, red, pink, and all shades in between. Both single and double flowers. The singles are preferred in the garden because the old flowers of the doubles usually hang on and spoil the appearance of the shrub. Will eventually grow taller than a medium-sized shrub, so should be kept pruned to garden size.   Planting Group 1

Osmanthus fragrans   Zone 8

(Sweet Olive)

219 One of the best of the *Osmanthus* family if kept to a 5 or 6 ft shrub. Tiny, fragrant, white flowers are hidden by the foliage on this exceptionally clean-looking shrub. Fragrance is much heavier in the warmer climates. Likes partial shade but will take full sun on the coast.   Planting Group 1

Osmanthus delavayi   Zone 7

218 Tiny, dark, glossy green foliage. In the spring, this plant is covered with small, white flowers on graceful, arching branches. They have a delightful, spicy fragrance. Wants slightly acid soil and partial shade. Usually a 5 or 6 ft shrub but will grow taller if not pruned.
Planting Group 1

218 *Osmanthus delavayi*

219 *Osmanthus fragrans*

220   Osmanthus ilicifolius

221   Osmanthus ilicifolius 'Variegatus'

Osmanthus ilicifolius (O. heterophyllus 'Ilicifolius')   Zone 7
(False Holly)

220   A sturdy, erect bush with Holly-like foliage that is attractive and clean the year around. Grows to 6 ft, sometimes taller. Fragrant, small, white flowers in the fall.   Planting Group 4

Osmanthus ilicifolius 'Variegatus'   Zone 7
(O. heterophyllus 'Variegatus')

(Variegated False Holly)

221   An evergreen shrub, seldom more than 5 ft. Dark green, spiny foliage with a creamy white edge. It is much slower growing and much more compact than O. ilicifolius. An excellent shrub to break the monotony of a heavy green planting. Best in partial shade and slightly acid conditions.   Planting Group 4

222   Philadelphus virginalis

PALMS
All Palms are listed in the Tall-Growing Shrubs section.

Philadelphus virginalis   Zone 4
(Mock Orange)

222   Deciduous. Medium-sized shrub to 6 or 8 ft, sometimes taller, bearing quantities of fragrant, white flowers in the spring and summer. Stands heavy pruning.   Planting Group 1

Philodendron 'Evansii'   Zone 9

223   An exotic tropical that does well in partial shade outdoors. Large, dark green leaves, 2 ft wide and as long as 4 ft. Stout, tree-like trunk with heavy aerial roots that reach the ground. Use indoors or outdoors.   Planting Group 1

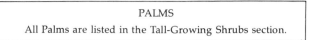

223   Philodendron 'Evansii'

224   *Philodendron selloum*

226   *Phormium tenax* 'Atropurpureum'

225   *Phormium tenax*

Philodendron selloum   Zone 9

(Split Leaf Philodendron)

224   Another lush tropical plant with deeply lobed, elephant-ear leaves up to 2 ft across. If you have room, plant in clumps, 3 ft apart for best tropical effect.   Planting Group 1

Phormium tenax   Zone 9

(New Zealand Flax)

225–226   Long, stiff, sword-like leaves. Does as well in the desert as on the coast. A number of varieties are available in the nurseries, some excellent for a tropical or Oriental planting. Other varieties: 'Variegated', 'Bronze', 'Rubra'.   Planting Group 1

227   *Pieris formosa forrestii*

Pieris formosa forrestii   Zone 8
(*P. forrestii*)

(Chinese Andromeda)

227   More vigorous than *P. japonica*. Leaves are longer and wider, and the flowers are three times the size. The most interesting feature of this plant is the brilliant red color of the new foliage. Sometimes the plant will grow taller but is best kept to under 8 ft. Same culture as Rhododendrons.   Planting Group 5

228   *Pieris japonica*

231   *Pieris japonica* 'Variegata'

230   *Pieris japonica* 'Flamingo Pink'

Pieris japonica   Zone 5
(Lily-of-the-Valley Shrub)

228   An attractive shrub up to 6 ft with dainty, white, bell-shaped flowers reminding one of a Lily-of-the-Valley. Needs excellent drainage, at least partial or full shade, plenty of peat moss, leaf mold, and acid food. Does not like the heat.   Planting Group 5

Pieris japonica 'Flame of the Forest'
                                     Zone 6

229   A new cross between *P. forrestii* and *P. japonica*. Has the many good qualities of the new, bright red foliage of *P. forrestii* and the white flower clusters and compactness of *P. japonica*. Plant in heavy peat moss.   Planting Group 5

Pieris japonica 'Flamingo Pink'   Zone 5

230   Same foliage, same size as the popular *P. japonica* and needs the same culture. The flowers are a nice shade of pink. Certainly an addition to the garden.   Planting Group 5

Pieris japonica 'Variegata'   Zone 5

231   Very similar to *P. japonica* but with striking, green leaves edged in white.   Planting Group 5

229   *Pieris japonica* 'Flame of the Forest'

232   *Pittosporum tobira*

235   *Poinciana gilliesii*

233   *Pittosporum tobira* 'Variegata'

234   *Plumbago capensis*

Pittosporum tobira   Zone 8

(Japanese Pittosporum)

232   The most widely planted of the *Pittosporum* family. Will grow higher than 6 ft, but should be held there or lower by pruning. Foliage dark green and leathery in either sun or shade, flowers are creamy white with a nice fragrance.   Planting Group 2

Pittosporum tobira 'Variegata'   Zone 8

233   Sport of *P. tobira* that can easily be held to 5 ft. The grayish-green foliage is used very effectively in flower arrangements. Prefers a dry location and will grow in either sun or shade.   Planting Group 2

Plumbago capensis *(P. auriculata)*   Zone 9

(Cape Plumbago)

234   Half vine, half shrub. Needs support. Left to itself it will mound up to 6 ft or more. Foliage is light green and the flowers are masses of pale blue. Needs little care. Full sun. Excellent bank cover.
          Planting Group 1

Poinciana gilliesii *(Caesalpinia gilliesii)*   Zone 9

(Bird of Paradise Shrub)

235   Shrub or small tree to 6 or 8 ft with light yellow flowers carrying brilliant red stamens and fine, feathery foliage. Needs heat, light, and well-drained soil.   Planting Group 1

236   *Prunus caroliniana* 'Compacta'

237   *Pyracantha fortuneana* 'Graberi'

Pyracantha fortuneana 'Graberi'   Zone 7
(Firethorn)

237   Strong-growing shrub with graceful, arching branches, covered with large, bright red berries. One of the best. Of all the broadleaf evergreen shrubs sold, probably the *Pyracantha* is in the Number 1 spot. Well adapted for espalier. Full sun and plenty of space for this 8–9 ft plant.   Planting Group 1

Prunus caroliniana 'Compacta'   Zone 7
(Compact Carolina Laurel Cherry)

236   The growth is slower and much more compact than *P. caroliniana,* making for a very desirable patio shrub.   Planting Group 1

238   *Raphiolepis ovata*

Raphiolepis ovata (R. umbellata)   Zone 7
(Round Leaf Raphiolepis)

238   Round, thick, leathery, dark green foliage on a compact, tough shrub to 4 or 5 ft. Flowers are white, in clusters, followed by blue berries. Sun or shade.   Planting Group 1

Rhamnus californica   Zone 8
(Coffeeberry)

239   A large, spreading shrub that will do well in either sun or shade and grow under very dry conditions. It has long, dark green, glossy foliage. White flowers are followed by green berries that turn red, then black, when ripe. One of the best California natives, but scarce in the trade.   Planting Group 2

239   *Rhomnus californica*

RHODODENDRONS

Another group of plants that deserves the honor of being called an "Aristocrat of the Garden." From Central California north, especially in the cooler coastal areas, Oregon and Washington, they are at their best. They have a wealth of beautiful, glossy dark green foliage and clusters of gorgeous flowers in the spring.

Rhododendrons are surface feeders and should never be planted any deeper than they were grown in the nursery. The hole should never be deeper than the ball but, especially in heavy soils, at least 3 ft in diameter. Throw out the heavy soil and make a mixture of peat moss, leaf mold, or compost, mixed with a small amount of soil and use this to fill around the plant. None of this fill should be placed underneath the plant, as eventually this medium will rot and allow the plant to settle. (The roots that go down are anchor roots which go after water and are tough enough to penetrate shale.) The roots that make the plant grow are the surface feeder roots, hence, the need for loose soil around the plant. Plants with surface feeder roots do not like to be cultivated as this destroys the growing cycle.

The roots should be shaded from the sun, even in cooler areas; until the plant is big enough to cover the root area, it could suffer from sun on the roots.

I have found that a large boulder (6 in. thick and 18 in. plus around) placed on the sunny side of the plant helps. (If you turn over a rock in a dry field in the summer, it is always damp under the rock.) This method of shading also helps other plants that require moist, shaded roots, such as Japanese Maples, Clematis, Camellias, Azaleas, and others.

Following is a list of a great many of the Rhododendrons now available (but not in all nurseries). Dwarf and medium- and tall-growing varieties are listed together in this section, as with other families. Some plants will easily grow to 20 ft in one area and only 6 ft in another.

Rhododendrons should be fed when they finish blooming and also may be cut heavily to shape them at this time. Extremely heavy pruning, say a 20 ft plant down to 4 ft, should be done two weeks before the blooming starts.

240   *Rhododendron* 'Christmas Cheer'

240B   *Rhododendron* 'Vanessa'

Letters and numbers indicate hardiness rating as follows:

H1 hardy to minus 25°   H4 hardy to plus 5°
H2 hardy to minus 15°   H5 hardy to plus 15°
H3 hardy to minus 5°

	HARDINESS RATING
'A. Bedford'. Lavender with dark eye. Late May	H3
'Alice'. Pink. Early May	H3
'Anah Kruschke'. Lavender-blue. June	H3
'Anna Rose Whitney'. Deep rose-pink. Late May	H3
'Annie E. Endtz'. Bright pink. Early May	H3
'Antoon van Welie'. Deep pink. Early May	H3
'Betty Wormald'. Pink with purple blotch. Early May	H2
'Blue Bird'. Blue dwarf. Early April	H3
'Blue Diamond'. Dwarf, bright blue. Early April	H3
'Blue Peter'. Lavender-blue, dark blotch. Early May	H2
'Blue Tit'. Dwarf, bright blue. Early April	H3
'Bow Bells'. Bright pink, semi-dwarf. Early May	H3
'Britannia'. Red. Late May	H3
'Butterfly'. Lemon-yellow. Early May	H3
'Carita'. Pale primrose. Late April	H4
'Carry-Ann'. Bright strawberry red. Early May	H3
'Christmas Cheer'. Early, light pink. March.	H5
'Cornubia'. Large, brilliant red. March	H5
'Cotton Candy'. Very large flower of pink and white tones. Early May	H3
'Cunningham's White'. White. Late May	H2
'Cynthia'. Deep rose. Late May	H2
'Daphnoides'. Rosy lilac, dwarf. Late May	H2
'David'. Blood red. Early May	H4
'Doncaster'. Scarlet-crimson. Late May	H3
'Elizabeth'. Bright red, semi-dwarf. Early April	H3
'Eureka Maid'. Deep pink. Early May	H3
'Evening Glow'. Deep yellow. Late May	H3
'Everestianum'. Rose-lilac. Late May	H2
'Forsterianum'. Fragrant white. April	H5
'Fragrantissimum'. Fragrant white. Early May	H5
'Gomer Waterer'. Blush fading to white. Late May	H2
'Graf Zeppelin'. Bright pink. Late May	H3
'Harvest Moon'. Lemon-yellow. Early May	H3
'Impeditum'. Purple-blue, dwarf. Early April	H2
'Jan Dekens'. Pink, ruffled edge. Early May	H3
'Jean Marie de Montague'. Bright scarlet-red. Early May	H2
'J.H. van Nes'. Soft red. Early May	H3
'Lady Primrose'. Lemon-yellow	H4
'Lamplighter'. Large, red. Early May	H3
'Lavender Girl'. Pale lavender. Early May	H3
'Loder's White'. White. Early May	H3
'Lord Roberts'. Dark red. June	H2
'Mars'. Deep true red. Late May	H2

'Mme de Bruin'.   Bright red. Late May   H2

'Mme. Masson'.   White with yellow blotch. Late May   H2

'Mrs. A.T. de la Mare'.   White. Early May   H2

'Mrs. Betty Robertson'.   Large, yellow. Early May   H3

'Mrs. Charles E. Pearson'.   Pale blush-mauve. Early May   H3

'Mrs E.C. Stirling'.   Blush-pink. Early May   H3

'Mrs. Furnival'.   Light pink, deep blotch. Early May   H2

'Mrs. G.W. Leak'.   Pink, dark blotch. Early May   H4

'Ocean Lake'.   Deep blue, dwarf. Early April   H3

'Odee Wright'.   Yellow. Early   H3

'Pink Pearl'.   Pink. Early May   H3

'Purple Splendour'.   Deep purple, dark blotch. Late May   H2

'Queen Mary'.   Large, deep pink. Early May   H2

'Ramapo'.   Dwarf, violet-blue. Early April   H1

'Royal Purple'.   Purple, yellow blotch. Late May   H2

'Sapphire'.   Deep blue, dwarf. Early April   H3

'Sappho'.   White with purple blotch. Early May   H2

'Scarlet Wonder'.   Red, semi-dwarf. Late April   H2

'Scintillation'.   Pink. Early May   H2

'Souv. of W.C. Slocock'.   Primrose-yellow. Early May   H3

'Trilby'.   Deep crimson, dark blotch. Late May   H2

'Unique'.   Soft lemon. Late April   H3

'Unknown Warrior'.   Early bright red. Early April   H3

'Vulcan'.   Bright red. Late May   H2

Wilsonae.   Pink, dwarf.   H3

240C   *Rhododendron* 'Rainbow'

240D   *Rhododendron* 'Jean Marie de Montague'

240E   *Rhododendron* 'Sappho'

Did you ever hear of "Blossom Blindness"? Many think it is a good idea to buy Rhododendrons in bloom (and we approve) but many people become so entranced with the bloom that they forget what the plant looks like and, all too often, they go home with a tall, loose-growing variety when they need a compact-growing plant, or vice versa.

240F   *Rhododendron* 'Mrs. A. Bedford'

240G   *Rhododendron* 'Purple Splendour'

240H   *Rhododendron* 'Elizabeth'

240I   *Rhododendron* 'Mrs. Charles E. Pearson'

240J   *Rhododendron* 'Loderi King George'

240K   *Rhododendron* 'Unknown Warrior'

240M   *Rhododendron* 'Cilpinense'

240N   *Rhododendron* 'Rose Elf'

240O   *Rhododendron* 'Ocean Lake'

240L   *Rhododendron* 'Bow Bell'

240P   *Rhododendron* 'Pink Pearl'

240Q   *Rhododendron* 'Mrs. E.C. Stirling'

240R   *Rhododendron* 'Eureka Maid'

240S   *Rhododendron* 'Anna Rose Whitney'

240T   *Rhododendron* 'Mrs. G.W. Leak'

Rhus ovata Zone 9

(Sugar Bush)

241 Native California evergreen. Usually an erect shrub, 5 or 6 ft tall, and as wide. Nearly round, 2–3 in. leaves that are gray-green, thick, and leathery. The flowers are white or pinkish in dense clusters. Like its cousin, the Poison Oak (but no rash with this one), it will stand all conditions; drought or lawn water. Likes sun, poor soil, or good soil. Stands wind or salt spray. Adaptable to pruning. Really an excellent shrub. Planting Group 1

Planting Group 1

241   *Rhus ovata*

242   *Rhus typhina* 'Laciniata'

Rhus typhina 'Laciniata' Zone 3

(Staghorn Sumac)

242 Deciduous shrub or small tree with divided leaves, dark green above and grayish underneath, turning a rich red in the fall. Stands extreme heat and cold, garden watering, or drought.
Planting Group 1

243   *Ribes sanguineum*

Ribes sanguineum Zone 7

(Red Flowering Currant)

243 A very satisfactory, deciduous shrub. Usually grows to 6 or 8 ft, and is covered in the spring with deep pink to red flowers having a spicy fragrance. Planting Group 1

Romneya coulteri Zone 7

(Matilija Poppy)

244 One of California's finest natives for a dry hillside. Blooms are huge, snow-white, "crepe paper" flowers with a large cluster of golden stamens in the center, reminding one of a fried egg "sunny-side-up." Has gray-green foliage. Grows to 5 or 6 ft; spreads rapidly from underground roots. Planting Group 3

244   *Romneya coulteri*

245   Sarcococca ruscifolia

247   Spiraea prunifolia

Sarcococca ruscifolia   Zone 6

245   Medium-sized shrub to 4–5 ft, with equal spread. Dark green foliage with very small, fragrant, white flowers which are followed by small, red berries that later turn black. A shade plant that wants good drainage and only small amounts of water.   Planting Group 5

246   Spartium junceum

Spartium junceum   Zone 7
(Yellow Spanish Broom)

246   Excellent plant, both for the seashore and the hot, dry districts. The plants have slender, bright green, almost-leafless, upright branches to 8 ft, which are covered with fragrant, yellow flowers in the spring.   Planting Group 1

Spiraea prunifolia   Zone 4
(Shoe Button or Bridal Wreath Spireaa)

247   Deciduous. This double-flowered *Spiraea* grows to about 6 ft. Upright growth with graceful branches covered in early spring with small, double white flowers along the stem.   Planting Group 1

248   Spiraea vanhouttei

Spiraea vanhouttei   Zone 4
(Bridal Wreath)

248   Deciduous. In the spring, all over the country, *Spiraea* is prized for the tiny, white flowers that entirely clothe the arching branches. The bushes look like they are covered with snow.   Planting Group 1

250   *Syringa vulgaris* 'Lavender Lady'

249   *Syringa persica laciniata*

251   *Syringa vulgaris* 'Esther Staley'

Syringa persica laciniata (S. laciniata)   Zone 5
(Cut-leaf Persian Lilac)

249   Deciduous. Best of the Lilacs; adapted to the hot parts of the West. Fine, cut-leaf foliage and lavender flowers. Also grows well in the cooler coastal regions.   Planting Group 1

Syringa vulgaris   Zone 4
(Lilac)

250–251–252–253   Deciduous shrubs. Many named varieties and various colors: lavender, blue, pink, and white, both double and single flowers. All are best where winter brings a pronounced chill. They like an alkaline soil. Where soil is acid, work lime into the soil.
          Planting Group 1

52   *Syringa vulgaris* 'Ellen Willmott'

253   *Syringa vulgaris* 'Vulcan'

254   Ternstroemia japonica

255   Teucrium fruticans

257   Viburnum suspensum

Ternstroemia japonica (T. gymnanthera)   Zone 7

254   One of the finest landscape shrubs in the trade. Grows compactly to 5 or 6 ft (sometimes taller) and as broad. Handsome, dark green, Camellia-like foliage has a bronzy cast in the shade and a much bronzier cast in the sun, turning to red in the fall and winter. A relative of the Camellia, so give it the same soil culture.   Planting Group 4

Teucrium fruticans   Zone 8
(Bush Germander)

255   Light gray foliage and pale blue flowers almost the year around. It requires a hot, dry, well-drained soil.   Planting Group 3

Vaccinium ovatum   Zone 8
(Evergreen Huckleberry)

256   Native to hills close to the coast, from Monterey north to British Columbia. Erect plant with leathery, dark green foliage. Pinkish flowers in the spring, followed by berries that are blue-back and excellent for pies and jam. Best in partial shade. Cut branches popular with florists.   Planting Group 2

Viburnum suspensum   Zone 8
(Sandankwa Viburnum)

257   A handsome, dense shrub with glossy green, wrinkled leaves. Use as a specimen or hedge, as it is neat and attractive at all times. Sun or shade.   Planting Group 1

256   Vaccinium ovatum

Weigela florida 'Bristol Ruby' Zone 5

258 Deciduous. Well-known shrub producing masses of red flowers in the spring and summer. Prune after flowering to develop new wood for next year's flowers. Sun. Grows anywhere. Planting Group 1

258   *Weigela florida* 'Bristol Ruby'

Weigela florida 'Rosea' Zone 5
(Pink Weigela)

259 Deciduous. Large clusters of bright pink flowers in spring and early summer. This is the common pink variety well known all over the United States. Grows anywhere but does best in full sun and should be pruned heavily after blooming. Will grow to 10 ft, but should be pruned down to 5 in July, then allowed to grow.
Planting Group 1

259   *Weigela florida* 'Rosea'

Xylosma senticosum (X. congestum) Zone 8
(Shiny Xylosma)

260 Here is an excellent shrub for any place in the garden, tough or not. Takes a hot location or part shade. Excellent trained on the wall as an espalier. The foliage is light yellow-apple-green color. Will grow much taller than 6 ft, but best kept pruned to this height.
Planting Group 1

260   *Xylosma senticosum*

TALL-GROWING SHRUBS

Plants in this group usually grow to 9 ft or more. All are evergreen unless otherwise mentioned.

261   *Aralia papyrifera*

?62   *Arbutus unedo*

263   *Azara microphylla*

Aralia papyrifera (Tetrapanax papiferus)   Zone 8

(Rice Paper Plant)

261   Plant this for a tropical effect. It is tall and bold with greenish-gray leaves, often 15 in. across. It is difficult to grow anything underneath this plant.   Planting Group 3

Arbutus unedo   Zone 8

(Strawberry Tree)

262   The dark green foliage resembles the native California Toyon. When mature, the tree produces clusters of small, bell-shaped flowers, which develop into bright red "strawberries." Deer proof.   Planting Group 3

Azara microphylla   Zone 8

(Box Leaf Azara)

263   Tall-growing shrub or small tree with tiny Boxwood-like foliage. Fan-like branching makes it ideal to spread out against a high, blank wall. Sun or partial-shade.   Planting Group 1

266   *Bambusa phyllostachys* 'Nigra'

264   *Bambusa phyllostachys* 'Aurea'

Bambusa phyllostachys 'Aurea'   Zone 8
(*Phyllostachys* 'Aurea')

(Golden Bamboo)

264   This is the most popular variety of Bamboo. It grows to approximately 15 ft. Sun or shade. Good tub plant. The cost of Bamboo is usually almost double that of other plants, because nurseries cannot propagate it in the usual way. It must be grown, divided, then established again, making a double process of growing. Invasive, unless roots are restricted.   Planting Group 1

Bambusa phyllostachys 'Bambusoides'   Zone 8
(*Phyllostachys* 'Bambusoides')

(Giant Timber Bamboo)

265   The poles are up to 4 in. in diameter and will grow to a height of 30–40 ft if given plenty of heat and water.   Planting Group 1

Bambusa phyllostachys 'Nigra'   Zone 8
(*Phyllostachys* 'Nigra')

(Black Bamboo)

266   Grows to about 10 ft, with the poles turning black. Great favorite in an Oriental planting.   Planting Group 1

Beaucarnea recurvata   Zone 9

(Bottle Ponytail)

267   Native to the dry regions of Texas and Mexico. Likes a dry, exposed spot with rich, well-drained, sandy loam. Will stand dry desert conditions. It is a Dracaena-like plant with a tall trunk and swollen base. Excellent tub plant.
                     Planting Group 1

265   *Bambusa phyllostachys* 'Bambusoides'

267   *Beaucarnea recurvata*

268   Callistemon lanceolatus

270   Carpenteria californica

Callistemon lanceolatus (C. citrinus)   Zone 9

(Red or Lemon Bottlebrush)

268   Rounded shrub or small tree to 15 ft. Flowers look like bunches of bright red brushes in May and June, and again later in the season. Very showy; stands sun and drought. Also trained as a tree.

Planting Group 1

Ceanothus arboreus 'Ray Hartman'

Zone 8

271   One of the new hybrid varieties of *Ceanothus.* A small tree (to 15 ft) that can be maintained as a large shrub with some pruning. Large, dark green leaves and bright blue flowers, 3–5 in. long, borne in open clusters.

Planting Group 2

Callistemon viminalis   Zone 9

(Weeping Bottlebrush)

269   When used as a specimen, it makes a dense mass of brilliant, fire-red bottlebrushes. Grows to 15 ft and stands sun; does not like wind or a very dry area. Also trained as a tree.   Planting Group 1

Carpenteria californica   Zone 8

(Bush Anemone)

270   One of the finest California natives. Thick, dark green foliage that is white underneath. From June to August has white, 2 in., Anemone-like flowers. One of the natives that will take garden watering in the summer if it has good drainage. Very scarce.

Planting Group 2

271   Ceanothus arboreus 'Ray Hartman'

269   Callistemon viminalis

272   *Ceanothus cyaneus* 'Sierra Blue'

275   *Cocculus laurifolius*

Ceanothus cyaneus 'Sierra Blue'   Zone 8

272   Vigorous, large-growing shrub with dark green foliage and large plume flowers of bright blue in spring. Grows to about 10 ft, but can be kept pruned.   Planting Group 2

273   *Cercis canadensis*

274   *Cercis occidentalis*

Cercis canadensis   Zone 4
(Eastern Redbud)

273   Deciduous. Medium-sized, round-headed tree or shrub. Small, rose-pink flowers clothe bare, brown branches in early spring.
                                                         Planting Group 1

Cercis occidentalis   Zone 5
(Western Redbud)

274   Deciduous. Bush or small tree covered with magenta, Sweet-Pea-shaped flowers, followed by handsome, 3 in. diameter leaves. In the fall, it has "Autumn" color.   Planting Group 2

Cocculus laurifolius   Zone 8
(Laurelleaf Snailseed)

275   Excellent background shrub in the shade or sun. Will grow to 10 ft or more with graceful, arching foliage of a beautiful, dark green. Leaves are 4–5 in. long. Stands heavy pruning. Tolerates poor soil. Foliage good for flower arrangements. It is not used enough.
                                                       Planting Group 1 or 4

276 *Cortaderia selloana*

277 *Cotinus coggygria*

Cortaderia selloana   Zone 5

(Pampas Grass)

276 Giant ornamental grass. Very conspicuous plume flowers in pink or white that grow half again as tall as the plant. Grows in any soil and becomes a pest, as large clumps are almost impossible to dig out by hand. Not for the small garden. Fast growing; dry location.

Planting Group 1

Cotinus coggygria   Zone 3

(Smoke Tree)

277–278 A tall bush to about 9 ft and about as wide as it is tall. Grows best when under stress in poor or rocky soil. Seldom good in a highly cultivated garden. Foliage bluish-green with large clusters of fuzzy, purple hairs. Variety 'Purpureus', which is also shown here, has purple foliage throughout the summer. Both deciduous.   Planting Group 3

278 *Cotinus coggyria* 'Purpureus'

Cotoneaster franchetti   Zone 5

279 Fountain-like, arching growth to 10 ft or more and as wide; however, in poor soil without summer water, only to 5 or 6 ft. Small, pinkish flowers followed by orange-red berries borne in clusters.

Planting Group 1

Cotoneaster pannosus   Zone 7

(Silverleaf Cotoneaster)

280 Tall, graceful shrub with gray foliage and long, arching branches. White flowers followed by bright red berries. Can be used as a quick-growing, tall background or a screen shrub. It requires little attention or water and will stand unlimited pruning.   Planting Group 1

279 *Cotoneaster franchetti*

280 *Cotoneaster pannosus*

281   *Cotoneaster parneyi*

284   *Dodonaea viscosa* 'Purpurea'

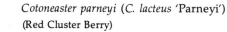

282   *Cyperus papyrus*

283   *Datura suaveolens*

Cotoneaster parneyi (*C. lacteus* 'Parneyi')   Zone 8

(Red Cluster Berry)

281   One of the best of the upright *Cotoneasters* with graceful, arching branches. It spreads wider (8 ft) than it grows tall. Thick, dark green foliage with heavy clusters of red berries that hang on most of the winter.   Planting Group 1

Cyperus papyrus   Zone 9

(Egyptian Paper Reed)

282   Tall, reed-like stems to 8 ft, topped by an 8 in. umble of lacy, thread-like grass. Plant in a wet spot; it is one of the few plants that can be planted in a fish pond. Very effective in an Oriental or tropical planting. Sun or shade.   Planting Group 1

Datura suaveolens (*Brugmansia suaveolens*)   Zone 9

(Angel's Trumpet)

283   Fast-growing evergreen shrub, sometimes a small tree to 8 or 10 ft. Large, 10 in. long leaves and lots of large, white, bell-shaped flowers about 8 in. long and 4 in. wide at the bottom, which continue to appear all summer.   Planting Group 1

Dodonaea viscosa 'Purpurea'   Zone 9

(Purple Leafed Hopseed Bush)

284   A fast-growing shrub or small tree from New Zealand. Excellent landscape effect is obtained when used as a tall screen and is kept thinned. It turns brilliant purple as soon as cold weather hits it. In the spring, it turns back to its natural rusty green. Different. Very interesting.   Planting Group 1

285 *Dracaena indivisa*

286 *Elaeagnus pungens*

287 *Eleagnus pungens* 'Maculata'

288 *Escallonia* 'Fradesii'

Dracaena indivisa (Cordyline indivisa)   Zone 8

(Blue Dracaena)

285 A tall plant associated with Spanish architecture but native to New Zealand. Grows to 15 ft and makes a striking effect with its narrow, lance-like leaves that grow as "topknots" on a thick, gray trunk. Plant singly or in clumps.   Planting Group 1

Eleagnus pungens   Zone 6

(Silver Berry)

286 Waxy, gray-green leaves above and silver and brownish underneath. Grows without care to 10 ft. Stands drought.   Planting Group 1

Eleagnus pungens 'Maculata'   Zone 6

287 Much more popular than *E. pungens*. The foliage is beautifully marked in gold. A fine, spreading plant that will stand drought, heavy pruning, and can be trained along a fence as an espalier.
           Planting Group 1

Escallonia 'Fradesii' (*E. exoniensis* 'Fradesii')   Zone 7

288 Medium- to tall-growing shrub to 10 ft, with a very compact, branching habit. Showy, rose-pink flowers in clusters from spring through summer.   Planting Group 1

289   Escallonia montevidensis

291   Eugenia myrtifolia

290   Escallonia organensis

Escallonia montevidensis (E. bifida)   Zone 7

(White Escallonia)

289   The tallest grower of the *Escallonia* group, often 15–20 ft. The foliage is glossy green, the flower panicles are white. Stands extreme pruning. Excellent on the coast.   Planting Group 1

Escallonia organensis (E. laevis)   Zone 7

(Pink Escallonia)

290   Excellent, tall shrub for background and screening. Flowers in large clusters of delicate pink to white. Not too good in salt-spray areas as the tips will burn.   Planting Group 1

Eugenia myrtifolia (Syzygium paniculata)   Zone 9

(Brush Cherry)

291   Much used in light, front areas as an accent specimen. Usually trimmed to a pyramidal shape. The new foliage is bronzy-red. Small, white flowers followed by ¾-in. berries of dark lavender. Extensively used for hedges and will make a nice tree to 25 ft if allowed to go untrimmed. Will tip burn at about 28°.   Planting Group 1

FERNS

All ferns, regardless of height are listed together in medium shrub section.

Feijoa sellowiana   Zone 8

(Pineapple Guava)

292   One of the best of the flowering and fruiting shrubs. This gray-foliage plant will grow to 10 ft, but can be easily kept at 6 or 7 ft. Flowers are white with bright red stamens, followed by edible fruit of a very delicate flavor.   Planting Group 2

292   Feijoa sellowiana

293 *Ficus benjamina*

294 *Ficus elastica 'Decora'*

Ficus benjamina   Zone 10
(Weeping Fig)

293 Outstanding, small evergreen tree or large shrub with rich, shiny green foliage of weeping habit. Used outdoors in the warmer areas of California and indoors elsewhere.   Planting Group 3

295 *Ficus retusa nitida*

Ficus elastica 'Decora'   Zone 9
(Rubber Tree)

294 Small tree or large shrub. One of the most popular indoor plants available, used outside in warm climates.   Planting Group 1

Ficus retusa nitida (F. microcarpa nitida)   Zone 9
(Indian Laurel)

295 Thick, leathery, rich green leaves on this handsome evergreen. Grown as a trimmed pyramid, a rounded patio tree, a globe, and as a large tree in warm areas.   Planting Group 1

296 *Fremontia californica*

Fremontia californica (Fremontodendron californicum)   Zone 9
(Flannel Bush)

296 A small native California tree or large shrub to 12 ft, requiring a dry location. Showy, large, yellow flowers are borne profusely in spring and summer. If watered in the summer it will grow vigorously for a year or so and then die.   Planting Group 3

299   *Hakea suaveolens*

297   *Grewia caffra*

Griselinia littoralis   Zone 9

(Kupuka Tree)

298   A tree in New Zealand and here a shrub to more than 10 ft, but we like it best when kept pruned to about 6 ft. Use as a compact hedge or windbreak. Will grow along the ocean, with or without water, but does best with water. Has dense, rich green, handsome foliage. Not too good in the hot interior.   Planting Group 1

Grewia caffra   Zone 9

297   Fast-growing shrub to 8 or 10 ft with a rather sprawling habit. A natural espalier. Easy to control. Prune often. The flowers are prolific, dainty lavender with yellow centers, from late spring to fall.   Planting Group 2

Hakea suaveolens   Zone 9

299   Shrub or small tree to 10 or 15 ft. The foliage is stiff, needle-like, and bright shiny green, even under drought conditions. Excellent on the seashore.   Planting Group 2

Hydrangea paniculata 'Grandiflora'   Zone 4

(Peegee Hydrangea)

300   Deciduous shrub or small tree to 10 or 15 ft. Leaves 5–6 in. long turn bronzy in the fall. Large, showy flowers in clusters about a foot long open white; then, as they age, fade to pinkish-bronze.   Planting Group 7

300   *Hydrangea paniculata* 'Grandiflora'

298   *Griselinia littoralis*

301   *Ilex altaclarensis* 'Wilsonii'

302   *Ilex aquifolium*

Ilex altaclarensis 'Wilsonii'   Zone 6

301   A bold, decorative shrub or small tree with large, thick, shiny green leaves and bright red berries. This Holly is self-fertile. Makes a good hedge or screen in both sun and shade.   Planting Group 1

Ilex aquifolium 'Variegata'   Zone 6

303   Golden, variegated form of English Holly. Green, spiny leaves with a gold edge. Very striking. Male and female plants required to produce berries.   Planting Group 1

Ilex aquifolium   Zone 6
(English Holly)

302   The traditional Holly of Christmas. A tall shrub or small tree to 20 ft, with glossy green, spiny foliage and red berries borne on female plants. Unfortunately, Holly berries are a sad subject for most nurserymen who neglect to tell their customers a male plant is needed for berries. Most Hollies are subject to scale insects so should be sprayed regularly. All will stand unlimited pruning.   Planting Group 1

Kolkwitzia amabilis   Zone 6
(Beauty Bush)

304   Deciduous. A beautiful 10–12 ft bush with graceful, arching branches and clusters of small, pink, trumpet-like flowers in May and June. Stands pruning. Likes sun but will stand some shade.
Planting Group 1

303   *Ilex aquifolium* 'Variegata'

304   *Kolkwitzia amabilis*

306   Lagunaria patersonii

305   Lagerstroemia indica

Lagunaria patersonii   Zone 9

(Cow Itch Tree)

306   A fast-growing tree or large shrub with a columnar habit. Two-inch, pink, Hibiscus-like flowers that have an interesting seed pod prized by flower arrangers. Excellent at the seashore.

Planting Group 1

Lagerstroemia indica   Zone 7

(Crape Myrtle)

305   Deciduous. Large shrub or small tree grown for its beautiful summer flowers. Colors are white, pink, lavender, and rose. Not good on the coast, where it mildews, or in the shade in the interior. When planted in a warm spot it is worth a space in any garden. Varieties:

L. i. 'Alba'	white
L. i. 'Purpurea'	lavender
L. i. 'Rosea'	pink
L. i. 'Rubra'	dark rose-red
L. i. 'Watermelon'	rosy-red

Planting Group 1

Laurus nobilis   Zone 9

(Grecian Laurel)

307   Wonderful, compact-growing, evergreen shrub. The leaves are the ''bay'' leaves used in cooking. Often grown as a standard or globe.

Planting Group 2

307   Laurus nobilis

309   Leptospermum scoparium 'Keatleyi'

308   Leptospermum laevigatum

Leptospermum laevigatum   Zone 9

(Australian Tea Tree)

308   Small tree with small, gray-green foliage and white flowers. Excellent as a screen or windbreak. Will grow and thrive under very trying conditions, even at the ocean's edge. Old specimens twist into interesting shapes with gnarled trunks.   Planting Group 2

Leptospermum scoparium 'Keatleyi'   Zone 9

(Pink Flowering Tea Tree)

309   One of the finest of the new group of *Leptospermum* hybrids. Will grow to 10 ft, but readily kept at 6 ft. The foliage is rather needle-like with large, open-faced, single pink flowers from December to April. Cut flowers are excellent in an arrangement. Wants a well-drained, sunny location.   Planting Group 2

310   Leucodendron argenteum

Leucodendron argenteum   Zone 10

(Silver Tree)

310   Large evergreen shrub or tree to 15 ft with silky, silvery white leaves that densely cover irregularly shaped branches. It needs fast-draining soil, will not grow in clay or alkaline soil, and it will not stand animal manure. Very scarce in the trade.   Planting Group 3

311A Magnolia campbellii

311B Magnolia denudata (M. heptapeta)

MAGNOLIAS

All Zone 6

(Deciduous Tulip Trees)

311 The Magnolias as a group, together with two or three other groups of plants, often have been called the "aristocrats of the garden." There are about a dozen varieties generally in the trade and all are somewhat fragrant. Any of them is worthy of the most favored spot in the garden. They like sun and well-drained, peaty soil, with plenty of summer water. They do not like drying winds in the summer or surface cultivation. All will make a tree in about 20 years. A few of the most widely distributed varieties are:

Magnolia campbellii

311A Huge, pink flowers up to 12 in. Many years before this variety will bloom.

Magnolia denudata (M. heptapeta)

(Yulan Magnolia)

311B/311K Large, pure-white flower.

Magnolia quinquepeta 'Nigra'

311C Dark purple flowers, pointed and cup-shaped, are pink on the inside.

Magnolia soulangiana

(Saucer Magnolia)

311D An attractive, large shrub or small tree that produces a very showy, lavender-pink and white flower before the leaves appear.

Magnolia soulangiana 'Lennei'

311E Saucer-shaped blooms, 8 in. across, purple-rose on the outside, nearly white on the inside. Fragrant.

Magnolia soulangiana 'Grace McDade'

311F Flowers very large, up to 10 in. across, deep purplish-pink outside and white inside.

Magnolia soulangiana 'Alexandrina'

311G Large, Tulip-shaped blooms, white inside, purplish-pink outside. A vigorous grower with large, rich green foliage.

Magnolia soulangiana 'Lennei Alba'

311H Vigorous growing with a large, globe-shaped, creamy white flower.

Magnolia soulangiana 'Rustica Rubra'

311I Deepest purple of all, white inside.

Magnolia 'Stellata'

(Star Magnolia)

311J The flowers are composed of many narrow petals, 3–4 in. across. White.

All Planting Group 1

311C Magnolia quinquepeta 'Nigra'

311D *Magnolia soulangiana*

311E *Magnolia soulangiana* 'Lennei'

311F *Magnolia soulangiana* 'Grace McDade'

311G *Magnolia soulangiana* 'Alexandrina'

311H *Magnolia soulangiana* 'Lennei Alba'

311I *Magnolia soulangiana* 'Rustica Rubra'

311J *Magnolia* 'Stellata'

311K *Magnolia denudata*

313   *Musa ensete*

312   *Melaleuca decussata*

Melaleuca decussata   Zone 9

(Lilac Melaleuca)

312   Large shrub that stands the windswept conditions of the West Coast. Tiny, ½ in. long leaves on arching, pendulous branches and pinkish-lavender flowers in abundance from May to September.

Planting Group 1

Myoporum laetum   Zone 9

315   Very large evergreen shrub or small tree. Fast growing to 6 ft or more the first year, later to 25 or 30 ft. Dense foliage or small, 1x3 in., dark, shiny green leaves. Very resistant to salt air and one of the fastest growing oceanside windbreaks. Not good except along the coast. Can be heavily pruned. Also trained as a tree.

Planting Group 1

Musa ensete (Ensete ventricosum)   Zone 9

(Banana Tree)

313   Here is tropical atmosphere at its best. Huge, long leaves (up to 8 ft long and 15 in. wide) with a heavy red or brownish midrib. Must be protected from strong winds which will shred the leaves; best planted against a tall wall or building. If you want it to grow fast, plant it with a full sack of steer manure in a large hole and keep it wet.

Planting Group 1

Musa maurelii (Ensete ventricosum 'Maurelii')   Zone 9

(Red Leaf Banana or Ethiopian Banana)

314   Huge, broad, tropical foliage. Leaves are wine-red underneath, as well as on top. Fast growing but must be protected from wind, as well as cold, as it tears easily.   Planting Group 1

315   *Myoporum laetum*

314   *Musa maurelii*

Osmanthus fortunei   Zone 7

316   A hybrid between *O. fragrans* and *O. ilicifolius*. Fairly slow, bushy growth to 7–10 ft. Leaves are spiny, ovate, and dark green. Excellent shrub in the shade but will take full sun in the cooler regions on the coast. Likes leaf mold and slightly acid conditions.   Planting Group 1

316   *Osmanthus fortunei*

PALMS

All Palms, regardless of height, are listed together.

Chamaerops excelsa (Trachycarpus fortunei)   Zone 8
(Windmill Palm)

317   Very handsome Palm. Trunk densely covered with black, hairy fibers. The crown is compact and the small, slender Fan Palm leaves form a thick mat.   Planting Group 1

Chamaerops humilis   Zone 8
(Mediterranean Fan Palm)

318   A multi-trunk Fan Palm forming a compact, green crown on each trunk. Very slow grower.   Planting Group 1

18   *Chamaerops humilis*

317   *Chamaerops excelsa*

319   *Cocos australis*

320   *Cocos plumosa*

Cocos australis (Butia capitata)   Zone 8

(Hardy Blue Cocos)

319   Stands more heat, frost, and drought exposure than any of the Feather Palms. Graceful, silver-blue, recurved leaf fronds. Retains its bushy form for many years and is an excellent tub plant for a hot, sunny exposure.   Planting Group 1

Cocos plumosa (Arecastrum romanzoffianum)   Zone 9

(Queen Palm)

320   Upright growth to 30 ft with long, graceful fronds. Rapid growing and does well in a landscape with other plants. It is used singly or in groups.   Planting Group 1

321   *Cycas revoluta*

Cycas revoluta   Zone 8

(Sago Palm)

321   Extremely slow growing, Fern-like in appearance. Usually considered a full sun plant but best with part shade. Attractive pot plant but do not overwater. Not a true Palm but a primitive plant that bears cones and is related to the Conifers.   Planting Group 1

322   *Erythea armata*

Erythea armata (Brahea armata)   Zone 8

(Mexican Blue Palm)

322   A tall Palm with a fine, spreading crown of rich silver-blue, fan-like fronds. Slow growing.   Planting Group 1

324   *Phoenix canariensis*

323   *Erythea edulis*

Erythea edulis (Brahea edulis)   Zone 9

(Guadalupe Palm)

323   The best Fan Palm. The large, fan-shaped fronds stay bright and fresh summer and winter. The spent fronds fall, naturally cleaning the trunk.   Planting Group 1

Phoenix canariensis   Zone 8

(Canary Island Date Palm)

324   A fast-growing Palm to 50 ft that forms an immense crown of dark green, graceful fronds. Too large for any but the big garden.
                                                 Planting Group 1

Phoenix reclinata   Zone 8

(Senegal Date Palm)

325   Probably the most picturesque Palm of all, especially when grown in a clump. The fronds are long and graceful.
                                                 Planting Group 1

Phoenix roebelenii   Zone 10

(Pygmy Date Palm)

326   A fine-leafed, small-scale Palm. Outdoors only in the warmer areas but a house plant everywhere else. A slow grower to a 10 ft stem with curved, Fern-like leaves on a dense crown. Needs moisture and good light indoors.
                                                 Planting Group 3

325   *Phoenix reclinata*

326   *Phoenix roebelenii*

328   Seaforthia elegans

327   Rhapis excelsa

Rhapis excelsa   Zone 9
(Lady Palm)

327   One of the finest container Palms but resents poor light, dust, and drought. Outdoors (it's hardy to 20°) it is best in the shade.
Planting Group 5

Seaforthia elegans   Zone 9
(*Archontophoenix cunninghamiana*)
(King Palm)

328   Tall, slender trunk with long, arching, bright green fronds.   Planting Group 1

Washingtonia filifera   Zone 8
(California Fan Palm)

329   Native of California. Large 4–5 ft, broad, fan-shaped leaves on this fast-growing, drought-resistant Palm. It grows to 50 ft or more.
Planting Group 1

Washingtonia robusta   Zone 8
(Mexican Fan Palm)

330   Tall, slender trunk, commonly swollen at the base, with brilliant green, fan-shaped fronds. Picturesque in appearance.
Planting Group 1

329   Washingtonia filifera

330   Washingtonia robusta

Photinia arbutifolia (Heteromeles arbutifolia)   Zone 8

(California Toyon)

331   California's most beautiful native shrub during the Holiday Season with its profusion of red berries. Takes garden conditions, although sometimes hard to establish. Very young, one-gallon-size plants are best to start. Try to pick a spot where there is perfect drainage.   Planting Group 3

Photinia fraseri   Zone 7

332   A very interesting, highly ornamental, fast-growing, vigorous shrub. Bright red stems and brilliant red juvenile leaves. Mature foliage dark green. Clusters of white flowers in spring. Mildew resistant. Also trained as a tree.   Planting Group 1

331   Photinia arbutifolia

Photinia serrulata   Zone 8

(Chinese Photinia)

333   Large shrub or small tree to 20 ft if not controlled by pruning. This shrub has a lot of good points and some bad. It has handsome, green, 4–7 in. leaves that are bronze when they first come out. In the fall the two-year-old leaves turn a fire-engine red and stay on all winter. In April, the plant is covered with 5–7 in. clusters of small, white flowers, by small red berries in the winter. The bad points are aphids and mildew. A regular spray program is necessary. Grows in full sun. Best in the interior.   Planting Group 1

Pittosporum crassifolium   Zone 9

(Karo Pittosporum)

334   One of the fastest growing of all the *Pittosporums*. Grows very rapidly to 10 ft, then, eventually to 25 ft. Gray foliage, ½x2 in., and maroon flowers in clusters. Drought resistant. Takes seashore conditions. Stands heavy pruning.   Planting Group 1

332   Photinia fraseri

334   Pittosporum crassifolium

333   Photinia serrulata

335   *Pittosporum eugenioides*

337   *Pittosporum rhombifolium*

Pittosporum phillyraeoides   Zone 9
(Desert Willow)

336   Large shrub or small, weeping tree to 15 ft that takes poor soil and extreme heat. Fragrant, yellow flowers in the spring.
                                                        Planting Group 1

Pittosporum eugenioides   Zone 9
(Tarata Pittosporum)

335   Erect growth. Tall, bushy plant with long, narrow, wavy, yellowish-green foliage. Excellent hedge plant or for screen to 15 or 20 ft. Any soil. Stands drought.   Planting Group 1

Pittosporum rhombifolium   Zone 9
(Diamond Leaf Pittosporum)

337   Another large shrub or small tree with diamond-shaped, light green leaves, white flowers, followed by orange and black berries. Best where there are mild winters.   Planting Group 1

336   *Pittosporum phillyraeoides*

338   *Pittosporum tenuifolium*

339   *Pittosporum undulatam*

Pittosporum tenuifolium   Zone 8

(Tawhiwhi)

338   Small, 2 in., light green foliage; used as a screen plant or excellent as a hedge plant. The best plant for a trimmed, pyramidal shape to take the place of *Eugenia* in the colder climates.   Planting Group 1

341   *Podocarpus gracilior*

Pittosporum undulatum   Zone 9

(Victorian Box)

339   Beautiful, large shrub or round-headed tree to 40 ft in the warmer areas. Rich, luxuriant, dark green foliage imparts a tropical effect. Very fragrant, creamy white flowers in the spring.
     Planting Group 1

Podocarpus gracilior   Zone 9

(Fern Pine)

341   Actually a Conifer. Soft, pendulous branches make this plant a delight to any landscape. Can be grown in the coastal sun, full shade, or in a pot indoors, and it is excellent as an espalier. Also trained as a tree.   Planting Group 2 or 5

Pleroma splendens (Tibouchina urvilleana)   Zone 9

(Princess Flower)

340   Velvety leaves and large (2 or 3 in.), purple flowers borne in profusion all over the plant, which grows about 8–10 ft tall and as wide. For weeks the ground underneath this plant is purple with the flower petals as they fall to the ground. One of the showiest of the subtropicals with rapid, somewhat leggy growth habit. Stands heavy pruning in early spring. It is worthwhile to plant in May as an annual in colder areas.   Planting Group 1

Podocarpus macrophyllus   Zone 9

(Yew Pine)

342   Slower growing than *P. gracilior*, with broader and longer, dark green leaves. Usually grown as a formal pyramid plant to 10 ft. Stands hedge shearing type of pruning. Excellent tub plant, either in the sun or shade.   Planting Group 2

340   *Pleroma splendens*

342   *Podocarpus macrophyllus*

343   *Podocarpus macrophyllus maki*

Podocarpus macrophyllus maki   **Zone 9**

343   This shrub has black-green leaves, smaller and more rigid than *P. macrophyllus.* It is evergreen and will grow inside or in full sun.
Planting Group 2 or 5

346   *Prunus laurocerasus*

Prunus caroliniana   **Zone 8**

(Carolina Laurel Cherry)

344   Large shrub or small tree ideal for screen planting or specimen shrub. Glossy, light green foliage and small, white flowers followed by black cherries.   Planting Group 1

Prunus ilicifolia   **Zone 8**

(Holly Leaf Cherry)

345   Tall shrub with Holly-like leaves useful for background planting or a screening. Wants dry, well-drained soil and full sun.
Planting Group 2

Prunus laurocerasus   **Zone 7**

(English Laurel)

346   Fast-growing shrub, or small tree to 20 ft if not pruned. Grown as a foundation shrub, if kept to 6 or 8 ft. The leaves are thick and leathery and always have a fresh, green look. Sun or shade.   Planting Group 1

344   *Prunus caroliniana*

345   *Prunus ilicifolia*

347 *Prunus lusitanica*

348 *Prunus lyonii*

Prunus lusitanica   Zone 7
(Portugal Laurel)

347 Slower growing than English Laurel and the leaves are much smaller. Makes a dense shrub, usually not more than 8 ft or so, but can become much larger. Stands unlimited pruning. Any soil. Sun or shade.   Planting Group 1

Punica granatum   Zone 7
(Pomegranate)

350 Deciduous tree or large shrub. Showy, orange-red flowers, some varieties producing Pomegranates. Narrow, glossy, bright green leaves. Best in the warmest areas.
     Planting Group 1

Prunus lyonii   Zone 8
(Catalina Cherry)

348 Leaves are as glossy as *P. ilicifolia,* but double the size (about 4 or 5 in. long) and fairly smooth. Excellent, tall hedge plant in dry areas. Prefers sun but will take some shade. Will stand very heavy pruning.
     Planting Group 1

Psidium cattleianum (P. littorale longipes)   Zone 10
(Red Strawberry Guava)

349 Large, evergreen, glossy-leaved shrub that bears edible, strawberry-flavored fruit. Very good for jelly.   Planting Group 1

349 *Psidium cattleianum*

350 *Punica granatum*

351 *Pyracantha coccinea* 'Lalandei'

353 *Rhamnus alaternus* 'Variegata'

Rhamnus alaternus   Zone 7

(Italian Buckthorn)

352 Excellent, fast-growing, clean-looking shrub for either sun or shade. Tolerant to heat, drought, or wind. Grows to 20 ft but stands pruning, so it can be kept tall and narrow.   Planting Group 1

Pyracantha coccinea 'Lalandei'   Zone 7

351 Tall growing with orange berries. This variety will stand much more cold weather and the branches are very stiff and upright.
                                        Planting Group 1

Rhamnus alaternus 'Variegata'   Zone 7

353 This one does not grow quite so tall or fast as *R. alaternus* but can easily grow to 10 ft and, like its parent, takes drought or garden watering, heat or wind, full sun or part shade. Keep the occasional green stems that show cut out.   Planting Group 1

Rhus integrifolia   Zone 9

(Lemonade Berry)

354 Evergreen. Leathery, nearly round leaves (to about 2 in.) on a shrub to 10 ft or more. Pinkish-white flowers followed by flat, sticky, dark-red fruit. A fine shrub.   Planting Group 2

352 *Rhamnus alaternus*

354 *Rhus integrifolia*

355   *Stranvaesia davidiana*

356   *Strelitzia nicolai*

Stranvaesia davidiana   Zone 7

355   A wide-spreading shrub to about 15 ft that is best if given plenty of room in the sun. White flowers in June followed by red berries and bronze foliage suitable for holiday cutting. Best in the Northwest.
Planting Group 1

Strelitzia nicolai   Zone 9
(Giant Bird of Paradise)

356   Tall, tree-like growth with large, banana-like leaves and large, bird-like, blue and white flowers in fall and winter. Excellent tropical accent plant.   Planting Group 1

Tamarix tetrandra (T. parviflora)   Zone 6
(Tamarisk)

357   Large, graceful shrub to 15 ft in height and 15–20 ft across with 2 in. long, pink flowers in clusters.   Planting Group 1

Tecoma capensis (Tecomaria capensis)   Zone 9
(Cape Honeysuckle)

358   This large, evergreen shrub or vine is mentioned also in the vine section. It is used as often as a mounded shrub as it is a vine. Dark green foliage with bright Chinese-red clusters of trumpet-shaped flowers. Excellent at the seashore but it needs good drainage.
Planting Group 3

358   *Tecoma capensis*   357   *Tamarix tetrandra*

360   *Viburnum burkwoodii*

359   *Tupidanthus calyptratus*

361   *Viburnum japonicum*

362   *Viburnum macrocephalum* 'Sterile'

Tupidanthus calyptratus   Zone 10

359   A valuable, exotic, landscape plant in the warmer areas where it may be grown outdoors. This is a tall-growing plant with Schefflera-like leaves and an excellent, large, tub plant when grown indoors.
Planting Group 5

Viburnum burkwoodii   Zone 5

360   Large, dark green leaves on this hardy shrub to 8 ft. Large, waxy, pinkish-white blooms with a delightful Gardenia fragrance. Evergreen in much of California but deciduous in colder areas.
Planting Group 1

Viburnum japonicum   Zone 8

361   A vigorous, evergreen shrub to 8 or 9 ft with large, light green foliage. Fragrant, white flowers.   Planting Group 1

Viburnum macrocephalum 'Sterile'   Zone 4
(Chinese Snowball)

362   Deciduous in the colder areas but nearly evergreen elsewhere. Bright, glossy green, 8 in. long foliage, with flowers in clusters, 6–8 in. across. Blooms in April.   Planting Group 1

363 *Viburnum odoratissimum*

365 *Viburnum tinus* 'Robustum'

Viburnum odoratissimum   Zone 7

(Sweet Viburnum)

363 Grows rapidly to 10 or 12 ft and as wide. Handsome, 6 in. long, dark green leaves that have a varnished look. Some of the leaves, here and there all over the shrub, turn red in the fall. Fragrant, white flowers in spring and summer. Prefers shade but will grow in the sun on the coast.   Planting Group 1

Viburnum opulus 'Roseum'   Zone 4

(Snowball)

364 Deciduous. Well-known, very hardy shrub to 10 ft, producing masses of round "snowballs" in May and June. Another of the few plants that produces good fall color in California. Sun.   Planting Group 1

Yucca aloifolia   Zone 8

(Spanish Bayonet)

366 Slender, dagger-like leaves give this plant a very picturesque effect. Grows to 10 ft and has tall flower stems with showy clusters of white purple-tinged flowers in late spring and summer. Needs well-drained soil.   Planting Group 3

Viburnum tinus 'Robustum'   Zone 6

365 An excellent, dense-growing, tall shrub. In the winter, it is covered with clusters of pink buds which open to white flowers in late winter and early spring. It is taller growing and does not mildew like its parent, *V. tinus*.   Planting Group 1

364 *Viburnum opulus* 'Roseum'

366 *Yucca aloifolia*

367   Yucca gloriosa

368   Yucca recurvifolia

Yucca gloriosa   Zone 8

(Spanish Dagger)

367   Bright, gray-green foliage on this tropical-looking, multi-stemmed Yucca. Soft tips will not penetrate the skin. Overwatering may produce black areas in the leaves.   Planting Group 3

Yucca recurvifolia   Zone 7

368   A beautiful, bold, accent plant that loves a dry location. Long, showy, blue-green, recurving leaves on this plant, which branches with age.   Planting Group 3

TEMPERATURE RATINGS

Zone 10	40° to 30°
Zone 9	30° to 20°
Zone 8	20° to 10°
Zone 7	10° to 0°
Zone 6	0° to −10°
Zone 5	−10° to −20°
Zone 4	−20° to −30°
Zone 3	−30° to −40°

Temperatures suggested in this book are approximate. The growing conditions, for example, a warm, late fall, often will keep the plants from hardening off and a sudden cold snap has been known to freeze plants 20° above the normal freezing point.

TREES

370 *Acacia baileyana* 'Purpurea'

Acacia baileyana 'Purpurea'   Zone 8
(Purple Leaf Acacia)

370 Evergreen, attractive, purple-tipped variety of *A. baileyana*. Same delightful, yellow flowers but should be cut back regularly to keep producing the colored foliage. Excellent as a trimmed hedge.
                                                Planting Group 1

369 *Acacia baileyana*

Acacia baileyana   Zone 8
(Bailey Acacia or Fernleaf Acacia)

369 Evergreen. Small- or medium-sized, fast-growing tree with feathery, blue-green foliage. It is covered with a cloud of bright yellow, fuzzy flowers in the spring. Many asthma and hay fever sufferers are allergic to this widely planted tree. Grows anywhere.
                                                Planting Group 1

Acacia longifolia   Zone 8
(Sydney Golden Wattle)

371 Evergreen. A large bush or small tree much used as a background shrub or windbreak. Bright yellow flowers in the spring. Good at the seashore.   Planting Group 1

71 *Acacia longifolia*

372   *Acacia melanoxylon*

373   *Acacia verticillata*

Acacia verticillata   Zone 9

(Star Acacia)

373   Evergreen. Used mainly as a low hedge or tall bank cover to prevent trespassing. Pine-like, dark green foliage covers thorns and soft yellow flowers. Can be held at 4 ft as a bush but will grow to 12 ft if allowed. Withstands drought and wind.   Planting Group 1

Acacia melanoxylon   Zone 9

(Blackwood Acacia)

372   Probably the fastest-growing evergreen tree in California. It reseeds itself and grows to 40 ft or more. A goodlooking tree and, were it not for this bad habit of self-seeding, it would be more useful. As with the rest of the Acacias, weeds (or anything else) seldom grow under it.   Planting Group 1

Acer circinatum   Zone 5

(Vine Maple)

374   Deciduous. A slender but often robust, vine-like shrub or small tree to 20 ft. New foliage with reddish tints; leaves light green all summer, turning orange-scarlet or yellow in the fall. Likes a rich, moist soil. Native to Northern California or Oregon.   Planting Group 1

Acer japonicum 'Aconitifolium'   Zone 5

(Fern-leaf Full-moon Maple)

375   Deciduous. A small tree, almost shrublike, seldom more than 8 ft. The leaves are deeply cut with each lobe serrated. Excellent fall coloring. Should be planted where it gets some sun, even full sun, but with the roots shaded.   Planting Group 1

374   *Acer circinatum*

375   *Acer japonicum* 'Aconitifolium'

376   *Acer palmatum*

Acer palmatum   Zone 5
(Japanese Maple)

376   Deciduous. Small, bushy tree that grows rather slowly and gracefully. Leaves are small, 2 in., glistening green in summer, and rich shades of red or gold in fall. Ideal, small garden tree, but cannot stand wind. Can be pruned and thinned to give special effects. Resistant to oak root fungus, therefore, good as understory tree for Oaks.
Planting Group 4

378   *Acer palmatum* 'Sangokaku'

Acer palmatum 'Atropurpureum'   Zone 5
(Red Japanese Maple)

377   Deciduous. A small, gracefully branched tree or tall shrub. New foliage is brilliant red that deepens to dark red. Prefers shaded roots in hot and dry locations. Best in Northern California areas or farther north in Oregon and Washington. Of the selected varieties, 'Oshio Beni' or 'Burgundy Lace' are two of the choicest.   Planting Group 5

Acer platanoides   Zone 3
(Norway Maple)

379   Deciduous. Grows rapidly to 30 or 40 ft, eventually to 50 ft, making a handsome ornamental tree where there is plenty of space. It is a dense tree giving deep shade. New leaves in the spring are red; green all summer; then turns gold in the autumn.   Planting Group 1

Acer palmatum 'Sangokaku'   Zone 5
(Coral Bark Maple)

378   Deciduous. More tree-like than most varieties and in many ways very similar to *A. palmatum,* but smaller. The fall foliage is yellow with a tint of rose. The new growth and the bark are a striking coral red.
Planting Group 5

77   *Acer palmatum* 'Atropurpureum'   379   *Acer platanoides*

380   *Acer platanoides* 'Crimson King'

382   *Acer saccharinum*

Acer platanoides 'Crimson King'   Zone 3
(Crimson King Maple)

380   Deciduous. A patented variety of *A. p.* 'Schwedleri' that holds its deep red purple color until fall. An excellent tree where deep red color will accent the landscape.   Planting Group 1

Acer platanoides 'Schwedleri'   Zone 3
(Schwedler Purple Leaf Maple)

381   Deciduous. Purplish-red leaf variety of Norway Maple. Leaves stay red for a longer period than the regular Norway Maple but turn rusty green by midsummer.

Planting Group 1

Acer saccharinum   Zone 3
(Silver Maple)

382   Deciduous. The common name comes from the underside of the leaf which is silver-white, while the upper side is light green. Fast growing, to 50 ft, usually too large for a small garden. Tolerates, but is not too happy with, wet soil. Beautiful for a large shade tree.

Planting Group 1

Aesculus carnea 'Briotii'   Zone 3
(Red Horse Chestnut)

383   Deciduous. Rather slow growth to 20 ft; about as wide as tall. Large, divided, fan-shaped leaflets make a dense shade. Flowers are bright red plumes, to about 8 in. long, which stand upright above the foliage layer. Exceptional when in bloom.   Planting Group 1

381   *Acer platanoides* 'Schwedleri'

383   *Aesculus carnea* 'Briotii'

85   Albizia julibrissin

Aesculus hippocastanum   Zone 3
(White Horse Chestnut)

384   Deciduous. Moderate growth to 50 ft with a 40 ft spread. Large, deep green foliage makes a dense, round-headed tree. Hundreds of upright, white plumes held above the foliage in April or May.

Planting Group 1

384   Aesculus hippocastanum

Albizia julibrissin   Zone 7
(Silk Tree, Pink Acacia, Mimosa)

385   Deciduous. Grows rapidly sidewards to about 12 ft, then eventually to 30 ft, and spreads as widely into the shape of an umbrella. Does best where it has hot summers, not too good near the coast. Not a good patio tree because of the messy flower droppings.

Planting Group 1

Alnus rhombifolia   Zone 8
(White Alder)

387   Deciduous. Tall, extremely fast-growing, native California tree. Dense green foliage and gray trunk. Native habitat is next to a stream so plant this where it gets a lot of water.

Planting Group 2

Alnus cordata   Zone 5
(Italian Alder)

386   A strong, fast-growing, deciduous, 30 ft tree with a pyramidal habit of growth. Handsome, glossy foliage. Can be recognized by the catkins which hang on the tree.   Planting Group 4

386   Alnus cordata

387   Alnus rhombifolia

388   Arbutus menziesii

Arbutus menziesii   Zone 8

(Madrone)

388   Forms a broad, round-headed, evergreen tree to 100 ft. Bark very outstanding; a pale green changing to red. Flowers white followed by red berries. A wonderful tree for a wild native planting, but not too well adapted to general garden conditions.
Planting Group 1

Bauhinia purpurea   Zone 9

(Orchid Tree)

389   Partially to wholly deciduous. A very showy, 20 ft tree with umbrella-like crown. Slow growing, with large, 2–3 in., reddish-purple, fragrant flowers during winter and spring. Needs well-drained soil. Variety *B. candida* is white.   Planting Group 2

Betula alba (B. pendula)   Zone 2

(European White Birch)

390   Deciduous. A popular, fast-growing, pyramidal tree to 35 ft. Usually grown in groups of three or more. Lacy, light-green foliage and beautiful, white bark marked with black lines.   Planting Group 1

390   Betula alba

Betula alba laciniata   Zone 2
(*B. pendula* 'Dalecarlica')

(Cutleaf Weeping Birch)

391   Deciduous. Similar to the European White Birch, except that the main trunk is straighter, the branches are more weeping, and the leaves deeply cut. Usually planted in groups in lawn areas.   Planting Group 1

389   Bauhinia purpurea

391   Betula alba laciniata

392   *Betula alba* 'Youngii'

Betula alba 'Youngii' (*B. pendula* 'Youngii')   Zone 3
(Young's Weeping Birch)

392   A very decorative garden specimen that must be staked to the desired height as the branches hang straight down.
Planting Group 1

Betula papyrifera   Zone 2
(Canoe Birch, Paper Birch)

393   Deciduous. Similar to the European White Birch but more open in growth, not so weeping. The bark peels off in layers. Leaves about 4 in. long. Like the rest of the Birches, needs ample water during the summer and is susceptible to aphids so should be sprayed regularly.
Planting Group 1

Callistemon lanceolatus (*C. citrinus*)   Zone 8
(Red or Lemon Bottlebrush)

394   Evergreen tree to 15 ft that will take a dry condition and still produce brilliant red blooms.   Planting Group 1

393   *Betula papyrifera*

Callistemon viminalis   Zone 8
(Weeping Bottlebrush)

395   Evergreen. A fast-growing tree to 15 or 20 ft with pendulous branches and bright red flowers. Must be staked when young and is not for a windy area.   Planting Group 1

394   *Callistemon lanceolatus*

395   *Callistemon viminalis*

397   *Carpinus betulus* 'Columnaris'

396   *Camphora officinarum*

Camphora officinarum (Cinnamomum camphora)   Zone 8

(Camphor Tree)

396   Evergreen. Makes a round-headed tree not too large for a small garden, usually about 15 ft tall and as wide in 15 years. Eventually to 50 ft wide and as tall. Foliage light yellow green; very attractive, bronzy, juvenile foliage. Likes a dry location.   Planting Group 2

Carpinus betulus 'Columnaris'   Zone 5

(European Hornbeam)

397   Deciduous. Grows 30–40 ft in a dense, pyramidal form. Dark green foliage, 3–4 in. long, which turns yellow in the fall.
Planting Group 1

Catalpa speciosa   Zone 4

(Western Catalpa)

398   Deciduous. A round-headed, 50–70 ft, subtropical-looking tree. Extra large leaves and large clusters of 2 in. white flowers are marked with yellow and soft green. Well adapted to extremes of heat or cold.
Planting Group 1

Ceratonia siliqua   Zone 9

(Carob; St. John's Bread)

399   Evergreen. The "breadfruit" tree of the Bible. Rounded tree with dark green foliage to 20 ft and as wide. Ideal for street trees in drought areas. Must be in a dry location. With garden water the roots become shallow so it often falls over.   Planting Group 2

398   *Catalpa speciosa*

399   *Ceratonia siliqua*

400   *Chorisia speciosa*

Cornus florida 'Rubra'   Zone 4
(Pink Flowering Dogwood)

402   Deciduous. Grown for its spectacular autumn color as well as for the lovely pink "flowers" in spring. Use plenty of peat moss and leaf mold to ensure an acid soil condition. The roots should be shaded.
                                                                  Planting Group 4

Cornus florida 'Welchii'   Zone 4
(Tricolor Dogwood)

403   Deciduous. Flowers on this variety are a rather inconspicuous pinkish to white so is grown for its unusual, variegated foliage. The leaves, about 4 in. long with creamy white and pink variegation, turn to a deep rose, almost red, in the fall.   Planting Group 4

402   *Cornus florida 'Rubra'*

Chorisia speciosa   Zone 10
(Floss Silk Tree)

400   Evergreen to briefly deciduous. A spectacular tree in October, November, and December when it produces masses of pink blooms. When young, a fast grower, 3–5 ft a year, then slowly to 40 ft. The trunk, usually grass-green, turns gray with age and studded with spines. Fast drainage is the key to making this one grow.
                                                                  Planting Group 3

Cornus florida   Zone 4
(White Flowering Dogwood)

401   Deciduous. Small tree or large shrub for a shaded location. Likes a woodsy soil that is well-drained and has plenty of water. White "flowers" in early spring. Grown as much for the brilliant fall coloring as for the flowers.   Planting Group 4

401   *Cornus florida*

403   *Cornus florida 'Welchii'*

404   *Cornus nuttallii*

406   *Crataegus cordata*

Cornus nuttallii   Zone 7

(Pacific or Western Dogwood)

404   Deciduous. One of the most spectacular Western natives but not nearly so easy to grow as the Eastern Dogwood (*C. florida*). If you have an area where there is exceptionally good drainage, very little summer water, and shade so the bark will not burn, it is well worthwhile. Will grow to 30 ft or more.   Planting Group 3

Cornus nuttallii 'Goldspot'   Zone 7

(Goldspot Dogwood)

405   Deciduous. Leaves are splashed with bright golden spots. A long, 2 month flowering season and often another one in the fall. This variety blooms even as a 2 ft plant.   Planting Group 3

Crataegus cordata (C. phaenopyrum)   Zone 4

(Washington Thorn)

406   Deciduous. White flowers in spring followed by clusters of small, red berries similar to Pyracantha "berries" in the fall. Grows to 20 ft.   Planting Group 1

Crataegus lavallei   Zone 4

(Carrierei Hawthorn)

407   Deciduous. This variety grows erect to 25 ft and does not spread widely. Large, dark green leaves, 3–4 in. long and 1 in. wide. It is noted for its clusters of orange-red, cherry-sized berries that hang on all winter.   Planting Group 1

405   *Cornus nuttalii* 'Goldspot'

407   *Crataegus lavallei*

409   *Cupaniopsis anacardioides*

408   *Crataegus oxyacantha* 'Paulii'

Crataegus oxyacantha 'Paulii'   Zone 4
(*C. laevigata* 'Coccinea Flore Pleno')

(Paul's Scarlet Hawthorn)

408   Deciduous. The most popular of the flowering Hawthorn family. Long sprays of double red flowers in April. Some red berries in the fall. Grows to about 25 ft.   Planting Group 1

Cupaniopsis anacardioides   Zone 9

(Carrotwood)

409   Evergreen. An ideal tree for subtropical gardens. It is a clean tree, handsome in a patio, lawn, or as a street tree. The compound leaves are made up of 6–10, 4 in. leaflets. Fragrant, greenish-white flowers that turn to reddish seed pods. Stands salt wind on the coast or hot, dry winds inland and grows to about 40 ft.   Planting Group 1

Dodonaea viscosa 'Purpurea'   Zone 8
(Purple Leafed Hopseed Bush)

411   Evergreen shrub or tree. Attractive, fast-growing, small tree (or shrub) to 15 ft, having rusty green foliage that turns to brilliant purple as soon as the cold weather arrives.
                                        Planting Group 1

Diospyros kaki   Zone 8
(Persimmon)

410   Deciduous. Varieties: 'Hachiya', 'Fuyu', and others. Fruit trees have been excluded from this list, but, as it is one of my favorite ornamental garden trees, I have given it a place. A round-headed tree to 15 ft with a 20 ft spread. Immense leaves to 4 in. wide and 10 in. long that first hide the fruit, then turn into bright orange and red autumn shades. They fall, exposing the beautiful, salmon-orange fruit that stays on the tree until late November, when it is picked and allowed to ripen.   Planting Group 1

411   *Dodonaea viscosa* 'Purpurea'

410   *Diospyros kaki*

412   *Eriobotrya deflexa*

418   *Eucalyptus globulus 'Compacta'*

413   *Eriobotrya japonica*

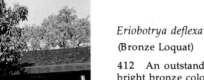

414   *Eucalpytus citriodora*

Eriobotrya deflexa   Zone 9
(Bronze Loquat)

412   An outstanding evergreen tree to 15 ft. The new foliage is a bright bronze color, while mature leaves are dark green.
                                                              Planting Group 1

Eriobotrya japonica   Zone 8
(Loquat)

413   Evergreen. Tropical fruit tree. Leathery leaves to 12 in. long and 4 in. wide; 15 ft high with equal spread. Edible, yellow-orange fruit in the spring. Unfortunately, almost all plants in the trade today are seedlings, and the quality of fruit from one plant to another is uncertain. It is very worthwhile as an ornamental tree. Pest-free.
                                                              Planting Group 1

Eucalpytus citriodora   Zone 9
(Lemon Scented Gum)

414   Evergreen. Moderate growth to 50 or 60 ft. A very slender and graceful tree with a beautiful, pinkish-gray trunk. Often used in groups of three, as with Birch, to get a full effect.   Planting Group 1

416   *Eucalyptus ficifolia*

415   *Eucalyptus ficifolia*

Eucalyptus ficifolia   Zone 9

(Red Flowering Gum)

415–416   Evergreen. A wonderful, small Eucalyptus to 25 ft. Great clusters of feathery, scarlet flowers. All are seedling grown, and even from selected seed a small percentage will bloom pink, white, or even orange. They do not usually bloom in containers, and, because of this, nurseries cannot guarantee the color. Be careful in transplanting, as this tree resents being disturbed and readily dies if the ball is broken.

Planting Group 2

Eucalyptus globulus 'Compacta'   Zone 9

(Dwarf Blue Gum)

418   Evergreen. A dwarf, compact form of the big variety so widely planted in California. This one is used extensively for a tall hedge or wind screen spaced 4–8 ft apart. Grows to 20 or 30 ft. It is bushy, has blue-gray foliage, and makes a fast screen.   Planting Group 2

Eucalyptus globulus   Zone 9

(Blue Gum)

417   Evergreen. A big, robust tree widely planted on Northern California hillsides in the early 1900's. Grows to 150 ft or more and, as cities stretch out into the hill areas, more and more are found around new homes where it is almost impossible to grow an ordinary garden because of the roots.   Planting Group 1

Eucalyptus lehmannii   Zone 9

(Bushy Yate)

419   Evergreen. Winter flowering, multistem with attractive, gray-green foliage and smooth, white bark. Excellent low screen tree that can be kept under 10 ft.   Planting Group 1

417   *Eucalyptus globulus*

419   *Eucalyptus lehmannii*

420   *Eucalyptus polyanthemos*

423   *Eucalyptus viminalis*

Eucalyptus pulverulenta   Zone 9
(Dollar Leaf Gum)

421   Evergreen. Moderate growth to 25 ft. Round, silver-gray leaves. Best when cut back for new growth. Extensively grown for the florist trade as it is very popular for use in arrangements.   Planting Group 2

Eucalyptus polyanthemos   Zone 9
(Red Box Gum)

420   Evergreen. Small, graceful, slender tree with dollar-sized, round, silver-gray foliage. All the foliage is widely used for indoor decoration. Should be heavily pruned and kept below 10 ft.   Planting Group 2

Eucalyptus sideroxylon 'Rosea'   Zone 9
(Red Iron Bark)

422   Evergreen. Slow, moderate growth to 40 ft. The tree is slim and airy in appearance with bluish-green foliage turning bronze in the winter. Masses of pink blossoms in spring and summer.
                                                  Planting Group 2

421   *Eucalyptus pulverulenta*

422   *Eucalyptus sideroxylon* 'Rosea'

426   *Fagus sylvatica* 'Tricolor'

424   *Fagus sylvatica*

Eucalyptus viminalis   Zone 8

(Ribbon Gum)

423   Evergreen. A fast-growing, graceful tree with pendulous, white flowers and very attractive, smooth, white bark.   Planting Group 1

Fagus sylvatica 'Tricolor'   Zone 4

(Tricolor Beech)

426   Deciduous. Glossy green leaves marked with white and edged pink. Slow to about 25 ft. The trunk burns in very hot sun or warm, dry winds. Do not allow it to completely dry out.
Planting Group 1

Fagus sylvatica   Zone 4

(European Beech)

424   Deciduous tree to 70 ft with a broad cone on top, while the lower branches reach to the ground. The foliage is dark glossy green. A good lawn tree but needs space to look its best.   Planting Group 1

Fagus sylvatica 'Atropunicea'   Zone 4

(Copper Beech)

425   Deciduous. Good in all except the hot interior, where the trunk is subject to sun burn. Valuable because of its purple foliage. All plants in the trade are grafted and a mature tree may reach 50 ft.
Planting Group 1

425   *Fagus sylvatica* 'Atropunicea'

428   Ficus elastica 'Decora'

427   Ficus benjamina

| *Ficus benjamina* | Zone 10 |

(Weeping Fig)

427   Evergreen. An outstanding *Ficus* that can grow outdoors in full sun in parts of California or grown indoors elsewhere. Will stand pruning. It has rich green foliage and pleasing, weeping appearance. Excellent container plant.   Planting Group 1

| *Ficus elastica 'Decora'* | Zone 9 |

(Rubber Tree)

428   Evergreen. Usually grown indoors except in Southern California, and known as the Rubber Tree. Large, bold, glossy dark green leaves. Excellent when planted in protected areas or as a tubbed plant.   Planting Group 2

| *Ficus retusa nitida (F. microcarpa nitida)* | Zone 9 |

(Indian Laurel)

429   Evergreen. Excellent, small tree for street use or as a tubbed specimen. Often grown as a pyramid or a patio tree (globe). Handsome, thick, rubbery, green foliage. Stands pruning. In Southern California many trees will reach 30 ft.   Planting Group 2

| *Fraxinus uhdei* | Zone 9 |

(Shamel Ash)

430   Evergreen. Excellent, fast-growing, round-headed shade tree to 40 ft. Has dark, glossy green leaves. Do not plant near a sidewalk as this plant is shallow-rooted.
                                                       Planting Group 2

Flowering Cherry   See *Prunus*
Flowering Crab Apple   See *Malus*
Flowering Peach   See *Prunus*
Flowering Plum   See *Prunus*

429   Ficus retusa nitida

430   Fraxinus uhdei

431 *Fraxinus velutina* 'Glabra'

Fraxinus velutina 'Glabra'   Zone 6
(Modesto Ash)

431   Medium-sized deciduous tree to 50 ft. A sturdy, fast-growing, round-headed tree especially suited for warmer areas as a shade tree. Fall bonus with this tree as leaves turn to golden yellow before dropping.   Planting Group 1

Gleditsia triacanthos inermis   Zone 4
(Honey Locust)

433   Deciduous. A thornless, fast-growing, slender tree to 70 ft. Excellent for the desert or any harsh growing location where it is hot.
Planting Group 1

Gleditsia triacanthos 'Moraine'   Zone 4
(Moraine Locust)

434   Deciduous. One of the fastest-growing shade trees (to 50 ft) in the trade today. Ideal hot-country shade tree, some flowers, clean habits and good form.   Planting Group 1

432   *Ginkgo biloba*

Ginkgo biloba   Zone 4
(Maidenhair Tree)

432   Deciduous. Large tree with spreading, open habit to 70 ft but usually only about 40 ft. Leaves are flat and fan-shaped, soft clear green in color, turning to soft yellow in the fall. Many trees sold in nurseries are seedlings. The females develop fruit in sufficient quantities to cover the ground. The fruit has a very disagreeable odor and is very messy. One should buy a named variety such as 'Autumn Gold' or 'Palo Alto' which are grafted and are male plants with excellent color in the fall but without messy fruit drop.   Planting Group 1

433 *Gleditsia triacanthos inermis*

434   *Gleditsia triacanthos* 'Moraine'

435   *Gleditsia triacanthos* 'Shademaster'

436   *Gleditsia triacanthos* 'Sunburst'

Gleditsia triacanthos 'Shademaster'   Zone 4

(Shademaster Locust)

435   Deciduous. This large shade tree needs plenty of room. It is as hardy and as tolerant as the other Honey Locust but grows faster, wider, and has larger leaves. Grows to 50 ft or more.
Planting Group 1

Gleditsia triacanthos 'Sunburst'   Zone 4

(Sunburst Locust)

436   A deciduous tree to 40 ft. This one needs full sun to be at its best and show its golden yellow crown of graceful, delicate foliage.
Planting Group 1

Grevillea robusta   Zone 9

(Silk Oak)

437   Evergreen. Tall, narrow tree to 60 ft with finely divided, Fern-like, deep green foliage. Four inch, golden yellow flower trusses are borne in profusion in the spring. Unfortunately, the tree drops leaves the year around so is somewhat messy.   Planting Group 1

Harpephyllum caffrum   Zone 10

(Kaffir Plum)

438   Attractive, fast-growing, evergreen, shade tree to 30 ft with luxuriant, dark green foliage. The new growth is tinted with red. Produces a small, dark red, edible fruit. Does best in warmer coastal areas and prefers light, moist, well-drained soil.   Planting Group 1

437   *Grevillea robusta*

438   *Harpephyllum caffrum*

441 *Jacaranda mimosifolia*

Hymenosporum flavum   Zone 9
(Sweetshade)

439 Evergreen. Small tree to 20 ft or large shrub with a slender, upright habit of growth. Shiny, dark green foliage and clusters of very fragrant light orange flowers in the early summer. Somewhat tender.
Planting Group 3

439 *Hymenosporum flavum*

Ilex altaclarensis 'Wilsonii'   Zone 6

440 One of the finest, large, evergreen, Hollies. Large, dark green foliage, spiny, thick leaves and large, bright red berries. Ideal as a large shrub or small tree. Planting Group 1

Koelreuteria bipinnata   Zone 8
(Chinese Flame Tree)

442 Slow to moderate growth to 30 ft and spreading. Leaves 2 ft long divided into leaflets. Flowers turn into capsules about 2 in. long and hang in large clusters about a foot in diameter and 2 ft long. Very showy in late summer and fall. Deep rooted and a good tree to plant under. Planting Group 1

Jacaranda mimosifolia   Zone 9
(Jacaranda)

441 Semi-deciduous. Somewhat tender, medium-sized tree with Fern-like foliage and clusters of lavender-blue flowers. Likes a very dry location and sandy soil. Does not like wind. If you have the right location, this tree is spectacular. Planting Group 2

442 *Koelreuteria bipinnata*

440 *Ilex altaclarensis* 'Wilsonii'

444   *Laburnum watereri* 'Vossii'

Koelreuteria paniculata   Zone 6

(Golden Rain Tree)

443   An open-growing, deciduous tree to 30 ft
that turns a beautiful yellow in the autumn. In
July and August, long, 12 in. panicles of yellow
flowers make this a most interesting tree. Takes
heat, cold, drought, wind, or alkaline soil.
                                        Planting Group 1

446   *Liquidambar styraciflua*

443   *Koelreuteria paniculata*

Laburnum watereri 'Vossii'   Zone 5

(Golden Chain Tree)

444   Deciduous. It is best where it experiences a cold winter. Small,
narrow tree to 15 ft with bright green, compound (clover-like) foliage,
and long (10–20 in.) clusters of bright yellow flowers that remind one
of Wisteria.   Planting Group 2

Ligustrum japonicum   Zone 7

(Japanese Privet)

445   Another fast-growing, evergreen plant grown both as a shrub or
tree, seldom more than 20 ft. Attractive, deep green foliage and
fragrant, white flowers in the spring. (Causes hay-fever for many.)
Stands heavy pruning.   Planting Group 1

Liquidambar styraciflua   Zone 5

(American Sweet Gum)

446   Deciduous. What Easterners miss most in California (and the
natives do not blame them) is the fall coloring. The *Liquidambar* is one
of the few trees that we can depend on to give the beautiful fall colors
in red and yellow. Grows as a narrow pyramid with branches beautifully spread to 70 ft. Leaves Maple-shaped. Excellent for a lawn
specimen. Stands seashore.   Planting Group 1

445   *Ligustrum japonicum*

447   *Liquidambar styraciflua* 'Burgundy'

448   *Liquidambar styraciflua* 'Palo Alto'

Liquidambar styraciflua 'Burgundy'   Zone 5

447   This grafted variety has been selected and named because of its rich burgundy red color in the autumn.   Planting Group 1

Liriodendron tulipifera   Zone 4

(Tulip Tree)

449   Deciduous. Fairly fast to 50 or 60 ft; symmetrical with a straight trunk; dark green leaves. Flowers are greenish-white and cup-shaped. A very desirable shade tree but needs water in summer. Will not stand alkali or summer drought. Another tree with yellow or yellow-brown fall color in the southern latitudes.   Planting Group 1

Liquidambar styraciflua 'Palo Alto'   Zone 5

448   A strain selected for its bright red leaves. All plants are grafted, so slightly higher in price than the seedling-grown *Liquidambar styraciflua*.   Planting Group 1

Lyonothamnus floribundus   Zone 9

(Catalina Ironwood)

450   A wonderful, fast-growing native California evergreen tree to 30 ft, adaptable to coastal conditions only. Attractive, dark-green, Fern-like foliage. The reddish-brown bark peels off in long ribbons. The leaves keep when cut and are used in floral arrangements. The spent flowers hang on for a long time. It is wind resistant but should be planted in a dry, well-drained location.   Planting Group 1

449   *Liriodendron tulipifera*

450   *Lyonothamnus floribundus*

451   *Magnolia grandiflora*

Magnolia grandiflora   Zone 7
(Southern Magnolia)

451   Evergreen. Moderately fast-growing tree with very large, dark green, shiny leaves. Flowers are white, large, and waxy. One of the most magnificent trees in the trade today. Eventually a large tree with a 50 ft spread, but it takes about 15–25 years before it becomes too large for a city garden. Grows faster with lots of water if well drained.
Planting Group 1

454   *Magnolia grandiflora* 'Samuel Sommer'

Magnolia grandiflora 'Samuel Sommer'
Zone 7

454   Evergreen to 50 ft. Considered by many to be the finest evergreen Magnolia. The large, white flowers, up to 14 in. across, are extremely fragrant.   Planting Group 1

Magnolia grandiflora 'St. Mary'   Zone 7

452   Evergreen. A small, especially desirable tree that looks like *M. grandiflora*, but dwarf to 18 or 20 ft. Leaves glossy deep green above and brownish underneath, flowers up to 12 in.; flowering even when young. Likes summer water.   Planting Group 1

Magnolia grandiflora 'Russet'   Zone 7

453   Evergreen to 50 ft. Another outstanding variety with somewhat smaller leaves and rapid, pyramidal growth. The branches are more compact and the leaves are dense. The reverse side of the leaves are russet-brown.   Planting Group 1

452   *Magnolia grandiflora* 'St. Mary'

453   *Magnolia grandiflora* 'Russet'

MALUS

FLOWERING CRAB APPLE   Zone 4

All are deciduous and seldom more than 20 ft tall. These are some of the most spectacular flowering trees in the trade.

455	*Malus* 'Almey'	Single red flowers; scarlet fruit.
456	*Malus arnoldiana*	Broad, spreading growth with arching branches; flowers are single pink fading to white.
457	*Malus* 'Bechtel'	Soft green foliage; large, double pink blooms; last to bloom.
458	*Malus* 'Dorothea'	Semi-double pink flowers; yellow fruit. (Not shown.)
459	*Malus purpurea* 'Eleyi'	Purple-red blooms; red leaves.
460	*Malus floribunda*	Flowers fairly large, apple-blossom color.
461	*Malus* 'Hopa'	Fast growing, upright; leaves dark green with a brownish cast; flowers rose-red.
462	*Malus* 'Katherine'	Large, 2 in., double bluish-pink flowers.
463	*Malus micromalus* 'Parkmani'	Early, showy pink flowers; small, red fruit. (Not shown.)
464	*Malus scheideckeri*	Semi-double rose-pink; small, yellow fruit.
465	*Malus* 'Snowdrift'	Pink bud and large, single white flowers.

455   *Malus* 'Almey'

456   *Malus arnoldiana*

457   *Malus* 'Bechtel'

459   *Malus purpurea* 'Eleyi'

460   *Malus floribunda*

462   *Malus* 'Katherine'

461   *Malus* 'Hopa'

464   *Malus* 'Scheideckeri'

465   *Malus* 'Snowdrift'

466   *Maytenus boaria*

Maytenus boaria   Zone 8

(Mayten Tree)

466   Evergreen. Moderate growth to 15 ft, then slow to 20 or 25 ft. Long, pendulous branches remind one of a small Weeping Willow. Excellent, small garden tree.   Planting Group 2

467   *Melaleuca leucadendra*

Melaleuca linariifolia   Zone 9

(Flaxleaf Paperbark)

468   A small evergreen tree to 30 ft with bright green, needle-like foliage and fluffy spikes of small, white flowers.   Planting Group 1

Melaleuca leucadendra   Zone 9

(Cajeput Tree, Swamp Tea Tree)

467   Excellent evergreen tree to 20 ft or large shrub with a distinctive, spongy, light colored bark. Rich green foliage and slender spikes of white, yellow, pink, or purple flowers.   Planting Group 1

Melia azedarach 'Umbraculiformis'   Zone 8

(Texas Umbrella Tree)

469   Excellent, deciduous, shade tree to 40 ft in hot climates. Will grow almost anywhere, growing rapidly in average soils. Nice clusters of lavender flowers in the spring followed by green berries.
                    Planting Group 1

469   *Melia azedarach* 'Umbraculiformis'

468   *Melaleuca linariifolia*

471   *Morus alba* 'Fruitless'

470   *Metrosideros tomentosa*

Morus alba 'Fruitless'   Zone 5

(Fruitless Mulberry)

471   Deciduous. A very fast-growing tree to 30 or 40 ft with as wide a spread. Large, shiny, dark green leaves and no fruit. Stands heat, drought, alkali soil, and neglect. Prune carefully when young as rapid, spindly growth can lead to frequent breaking of brittle wood.
                                                                                                Planting Group 1

Metrosideros tomentosa (*M. excelsus*)   Zone 9

(New Zealand Christmas Tree)

470   Evergreen. Excellent tree for coastal planting to about 30 ft. Will stand the wind as well as salt spray and ocean salt water at the roots. Thick, glossy, oblong, attractive leaves, dark gray on top, gray underneath. Large, dark crimson flowers in clusters in June and July.
                                                                                                Planting Group 1

472   *Myoporum laetum*

Myoporum laetum   Zone 9

472   Evergreen. A fast-growing, large shrub often grown in tree form to 20 ft. Well adapted to windswept coastal areas and drought conditions. Has thick, leathery (almost succulent-like), deep green foliage.
                                                                                                Planting Group 1

Olea europaea 'Mission'   Zone 8

(Mission Olive)

473   Evergreen. Extremely drought resistant once established. Gray-green foliage and picturesque gnarled trunks on older specimens that reach a height of 20 ft.   Planting Group 1

473   *Olea europaea* 'Mission'

Oxydendrum arboreum   Zone 5

(Sourwood, Sorrel Tree)

474   Deciduous. The 5–8 in. leaves turn a brilliant scarlet in the fall. In the summer it has clusters of Andromeda-like, creamy white flowers. Usually found in the Northwest. Grows to 50 ft; needs acid soil.
                                                                                                Planting Group 1

474　*Oxydendrum arboreum*

475　*Photinia fraseri*

Photinia fraseri　　　　　　　　　　　　Zone 7

475　Evergreen. Grown both as a large shrub or small tree to 20 ft. The new foliage has brilliant red leaves as well as red stems. In the spring, showy clusters of white flowers. This variety is more mildew resistant than most *Photinias*.　　　　　　　　　Planting Group 1

Pistacia chinensis　　　　　　　　　　　Zone 7

(Chinese Pistache)

476　Deciduous. A beautiful shade tree growing to 50 or 60 ft. Leaves, similar to the Black Walnut, turn a vivid red-yellow and orange in the fall. It is best where it is hot and well watered in the summer.　　　　　　　　　Planting Group 1

Pittosporum undulatum　　　　　　　　Zone 9

(Victorian Box)

477　Evergreen. Small, round-headed tree or shrub to 20 ft or more. Dark green, glossy, 6 in. leaves; fragrant, creamy-white flowers followed by orange berries. Fast growing. Stands considerable drought. Must be trained to tree form when young.　　　　　　　　　Planting Group 1

476　*Pistacia chinensis*

477　*Pittosporum undulatum*

478   *Platanus acerifolia*

479   *Platanus occidentalis*

Platanus occidentalis   Zone 6

(American Sycamore)

479   A very rapid-growing, deciduous Sycamore with an unusually large trunk. This one is for the "country" only, as it does not like the city air; otherwise almost the same as the London Plane. Grows to 50 ft.
Planting Group 1

Platanus acerifolia   Zone 7

(European Sycamore or London Plane)

478   Deciduous. Large, handsome street or shade tree to 70 ft. Leaves are large, dense, and bright green. It is tough, rugged, and tolerant of almost any soil condition.   Planting Group 1

Platanus racemosa   Zone 7

(California Sycamore)

480   Deciduous. This California native, often up to 100 ft, has large, Maple-like leaves. It is not a thick, dense tree as is *P. acerifolia*. The bark is grayish and mottled. Often grown in clumps at an angle. Picturesque.   Planting Group 1

Podocarpus gracilior   Zone 9

(Fern Pine)

481   Evergreen. This Fern-like Conifer grows to a medium-sized tree and is one of the most graceful plants we have in the trade. Can be kept to any size desired by pruning and will grow in full shade or full sun or indoors but wants a well-drained location without too much water.
Planting Group 3

480   *Platanus racemosa*

481   *Podocarpus gracilior*

Populus nigra 'Italica' Zone 4
(Lombardy Poplar)

482 Deciduous. Fast and columnar to 75 ft or more. Excellent windbreak for farmland, but requires too much space for a city lot. Keep away from sewers and septic tanks. Beautiful in the fall when leaves turn bright yellow before dropping. Planting Group 1

PRUNUS

FLOWERING PLUM Zone 5

All deciduous. These beautiful Oriental trees come in many colors and varieties. They are best in the colder areas, require well-drained soil, and very little pruning. Planting Group 4

483 *Prunus cerasifera blireiana*
    Foliage reddish-green. A showy, double pink that flowers early. No fruit.

484 *Prunus cerasifera* 'Hollywood'
    Leaves dark green above, red underneath. Flowers pink to white. Good quality fruit. (Not shown.)

485 *Prunus cerasifera* 'Atropurpurea'
    Purple leaf. Single, delicate pink flower followed by reddish fruit. Flower has only a faint blush of pink in early stages then clear white as it gets fully open.

486 *Prunus cerasifera* 'Thundercloud'
    Deep purple leaf, single delicate pink blooms. Some fruit.

487 *Prunus cerasifera* 'Thundercloud'
    In flower. No fruit.

482 *Populus nigra* 'Italica'

485 *Prunus cerasifera* 'Atropurpurea'

483 *Prunus cerasifera blireiana*

486   *Prunus cerasifera* 'Thundercloud'

487   *Prunus cerasifera* 'Thundercloud'

488   *Prunus persica* 'Double White'

FLOWERING PEACH   Zone 5

Deciduous and seldom more than 15 ft in height. Identical in growing and habit to fruiting Peach. Heavy pruning when in flower or immediately after for a good show of flowers the following year. Many named varieties in the trade but usually found in nurseries as 'Double Red', 'Pink', 'White', or 'Variegated'; all in early and late-flowering varieties.

Planting Group 1

488   *Prunus persica* 'Double White'

489   *Prunus persica* 'Double Red'

490   *Prunus persica* 'Double Pink'

490   *Prunus persica* 'Double Pink'

489   *Prunus persica* 'Double Red'

FLOWERING CHERRY   Zone 5

All deciduous. Grown for the rich red foliage as well as the masses of early spring flowers. These medium-sized trees will adapt to almost any soil condition. Used as container trees for a patio or for a lawn or street tree.   Planting Group 1

491 *Prunus serrulata* 'Akebono' ('Daybreak')
     Single pale pink flower and spreading form. (Often called the most beautiful flowering tree in the world.)

492 *Prunus serrulata* 'Amanogawa'
     Columnar. Semi-double soft pink.

493 *Prunus serrulata* 'Beni Hoshi'
     Arching growth; vivid, single pink.

494 *Prunus serrulata* 'Kwanzan'
     Upright growth; large, double deep pink.

495 *Prunus serrulata* 'Naden'
     Upright growth; semi-double soft pink.

496 *Prunus serrulata* 'Shirotae' ('Mt. Fuji')
     Double pure white.

497 *Prunus yedoensis* ('Yoshino')
     Fragrant, single white, early.

498 *Prunus subhirtella* (Weeping) Double pink, drooping form.

499 *Prunus subhirtella* (Weeping) Single pink, drooping form.

499A *Prunus subhirtella* (Weeping) Double pink, arching growth.

492   *Prunus serrulata* 'Amanogawa'

493   *Prunus serrulata* 'Beni Hoshi'

491   *Prunus serrulata* 'Akebono' 'Daybreak'

494   *Prunus serrulata* 'Kwanzan'

495   *Prunus serrulata* 'Naden'

496   *Prunus serrulata* 'Shirotae' ('Mt. Fuji')

497   *Prunus yedoensis* ('Yoshino')

498   *Prunus subhirtella* (Weeping) Double pink, drooping form.

499   *Prunus subhirtella* (Weeping) Single pink, drooping form.

499A   *Prunus subhirtella* (Weeping) Double pink, arching growth.

501   *Pyrus kawakamii*

500   *Pyrus calleryana* 'Bradford'

Pyrus calleryana 'Bradford'   Zone 5
(Bradford Pear)

500   Deciduous. A vigorous-growing, dense-headed, medium-sized shade tree with rich green, wavy foliage and attractive, scarlet color in the fall. Dense clusters of white flowers in early spring. No fruit.
Planting Group 1

Pyrus kawakamii   Zone 8
(Evergreen Pear)

501   Evergreen. Grows fast to 30 ft and requires constant pruning to keep it attractive as a tree. This bad habit, of course, helps when the tree is espaliered against a wall or fence. Bright, shiny foliage and fragrant, white flowers. No fruit.   Planting Group 1

Quercus coccinea   Zone 7
(Scarlet Oak)

503   Deciduous. Grows to 60 ft or more with a wide spread and a light, open pattern of branches. Bright green, 6 in., deeply lobed leaves that turn brilliant scarlet in the fall. Likes deep, rich soil. Cut branches are sold by florists. A must if you want fall coloring and have the space.   Planting Group 1

Quercus agrifolia   Zone 7
(Coast Live Oak)

502   Evergreen. This native California Live Oak is slow to 50 ft. Leaves small, oval, and rich green. Requires a well-drained location and should not have much, if any, summer water. Around new homes one must be careful not to change the soil level and must be careful not to dam up a planting area with a driveway that does not provide rapid drainage.   Planting Group 1

502   *Quercus agrifolia*

503   *Quercus coccinea*

504   *Quercus ilex*

506   *Quercus suber*

Quercus palustris   Zone 4
(Pin Oak)

505   Deciduous to 80 ft. Dark green foliage turning to a showy scarlet in the fall. Large, symmetrical pyramid when young, open and irregular when mature.   Planting Group 1

Quercus ilex   Zone 8
(Holly Oak)

504   Evergreen. Moderately fast growth to 40 ft with round-spreading head. Clean, dark green, glossy foliage. Faster and straighter growing than the California Live Oak and rapidly replacing it in the nursery trade. Grows very well inland, as well as on the coast, where it stands salt air and wind. Almost pest free. Excellent street tree.   Planting Group 1

Quercus suber   Zone 9
(Cork Oak)

506   Evergreen. Native to the Mediterranean. The interesting thing about this tree is the bark. (This is the cork of commerce.) The 3 in., toothed leaves are shining dark green above and gray beneath. Needs good drainage and can take considerable drought when established. A good shade tree to 60 ft if in the right place.   Planting Group 3

Robina ambigua 'Decaisneana'   Zone 1
(Pink Locust)

507   Deciduous. Tall, rapid growing to 50 ft. A variety of Black Locust with long racemes or fragrant, light pink flowers. Tolerant of both summer heat and cold. Will stand any kind of soil.   Planting Group 1

505   *Quercus palustris*

507   *Robina ambigua* 'Decaisneana'

508   Salix babylonica

509   Salix matsudana 'Tortuosa'

Salix babylonica   Zone 5

(Weeping Willow)

508   Deciduous. Fast-growing, very graceful tree to 30 ft with long, drooping branches. Long, narrow, bright light green leaves. Be careful where you place this one as almost nothing will grow under it; the roots take everything. It has been said this tree will dry up a swamp. Keep away from sewer lines.   Planting Group 1

Salix matsudana 'Tortuosa'   Zone 3

(Corkscrew Willow)

509   Deciduous. Grows to 25 ft or more with the branches twisted into interesting spiraling, upright patterns. Branches, both with or without leaves, are excellent for flower arrangements.
                                                Planting Group 1

Schinus terebinthifolius   Zone 8

(Brazilian Pepper)

511   Evergreen. Medium-sized tree to 20 ft. Leaves are larger, rounder, veined, and darker green than *S. molle*, and it is a much better all-around tree in the garden. Useful for shade in a small garden. Does as well on the coast as in the interior. Takes lawn water.   Planting Group 1

Schinus molle   Zone 8

(California Pepper Tree)

510   Evergreen. Fast growing to 25 ft with picturesque, gnarled trunk and long, graceful, weeping branches. Hardy, thrives best in poor, light soil and where there is plenty of heat and little water.
                                                Planting Group 2

510   Schinus molle

511   Schinus terebinthifolius

512   *Sorbus aucuparia*

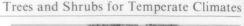

513   *Stenocarpus sinuatus*

Stenocarpus sinuatus   Zone 10

(Firewheel Tree)

513   Evergreen. Lovely tree to 50 ft that prefers an acid soil. Great masses of 3–4 in., wheel-shaped, brilliant orange-red flowers in the spring. Dark green, Oak-like foliage. Excellent for tropical gardens in warmer areas.   Planting Group 3

Sorbus aucuparia   Zone 6

(European Mountain Ash)

512   Deciduous to 60 ft. A tree best for the northern parts where winters are colder. Broad, flat, 3–5 in. clusters of white flowers followed by bright orange-red, ¼ in. berries which color in midsummer and hang on until midspring unless the birds get them. Needs good drainage; should have full sun but will take part shade.
                              Planting Group 3

Sterculia diversifolia (Brachychiton populneus)   Zone 9

(Bottle Tree)

514   Semi-evergreen tree to 30 ft with dense head and a nice, compact habit. The trunk, starting at the ground, is unusually thick. Yellowish flowers in summer. This one likes a hot, dry climate. Leaves always look a rich glossy green.   Planting Group 1

514   *Sterculia diversifolia*

515   *Tilia cordata*

518   Ulmus glabra 'Camperdownii'

Tilia cordata   Zone 3

(Little Leaf Linden)

515   Deciduous. A cold-weather plant. Small, leathery foliage, rapid growth in symmetrical form to 40 ft. Spicy, fragrant blooms.
Planting Group 1

516   Tristania conferta

Tristania conferta   Zone 9

(Brisbane Box)

516   Evergreen. A pyramidal tree to 50 ft that likes plenty of heat and withstands drought. Looks somewhat like a Eucalyptus. Fast growing, dark green foliage, and small clusters of white flowers add to its attractiveness.   Planting Group 1

Ulmus parvifolia   Zone 7

(Evergreen Elm)

519   Evergreen to about 23°, then deciduous. A 30 ft tree with a rounded-head and graceful, arching branches. Needs pruning every winter.   Planting Group 1

Tristania laurina   Zone 9

517   A slow-growing, formal, small tree or shrub to 10 ft. Leaves are narrow and about 4 in. long, making a dense, rounded crown. Flowers are clusters of yellow, borne in late spring. Evergreen.
Planting Group 1

Ulmus glabra 'Camperdownii'   Zone 1

(Camperdown Elm)

518   This interesting, weeping tree will grow to about 10 or 12 ft and as broad with branches that reach the ground, making a tent of shade. Very scarce in the trade.   Planting Group 1

519   Ulmus parvifolia

517   Tristania laurina

520   *Ulmus parvifolia* 'Brea'

521   *Zelkova serrata*

Zelkova serrata   Zone 5

(Sawleaf Zelkova)

521   Deciduous. Fast growth to 75 ft. Dark green, 2–5 in. leaves are sharply saw-toothed and turn red in the fall. Better adapted to the hot interior than the coast. An excellent, pest-free tree where there is room.   Planting Group 1

Ulmus parvifolia 'Brea'   Zone 7

(Chinese Evergreen Elm)

520   Evergreen above 30°F, then deciduous. This differs from *U. parvifolia* in its growth habit, being more or less in an upright, umbrella-like form rather than drooping and much stronger growth to 30 ft.   Planting Group 1

PLANTING GUIDE

Following each description is a planting group guide. Here again, individual conditions will vary so the planting instructions are general. An attempt has been made to give you a clue to the general soil conditions needed for each plant. You should check local conditions with your nurseryman.

Group 1 means the plant will grow in the sun without special treatment, unless otherwise mentioned.

Group 2 means the plant will grow in the sun, but must have excellent drainage.

Group 3 means the plant will grow in the sun, but must have excellent drainage and only minimum amounts of water, usually gray foliage plants.

Group 4 means the plant will grow in the shade, without special treatment.

Group 5 means the plant will grow in the shade, but must have excellent drainage and special soil mixture.

VINES

Ampelopsis quinquefolia (Parthenocissus quinquefolia) Zone 4

(Virginia Creeper)

522 Deciduous. A fine, fast-growing, deciduous vine with large, 5-fingered leaves turning brilliant scarlet in the fall. It will grow on any wall. Planting Group 1

Ampelopsis tricuspidata (Parthenocissus tricuspidata) Zone 4

(Boston Ivy)

523 Deciduous. Close-clinging vine especially suited to cover masonry walls. Pointed leaves with delicate, light green foliage which turns brilliant red in the fall. Planting Group 1

523 *Ampelopsis tricuspidata*

Beaumontia grandiflora Zone 10

(Easter Lily Vine)

524 A beautiful, vine for only the warmer parts of California. Large, dark green, 6 in. leaves are smooth and shiny and furnish a tropical look. Blooms from April until September with fragrant, trumpet-like, 4–5 in. long, white flowers that look like Easter Lilies. Needs deep, rich soil, ample water, and regular feeding. Evergreen. Planting Group 1

524 *Beaumontia grandiflora*

522 *Ampelopsis quinquefolia*

525   Bignonia cherere

Bignonia cherere (Distictis buccinatoria)   Zone 9
(Scarlet Trumpet Vine)

525   A beautiful, evergreen vine that will take only a light frost. Makes a very heavy, quick cover with clusters of 4 in., bright red, tubular flowers having yellow throats. Blooms sporadically throughout the year when the weather warms. Stands heavy pruning. Feed and water regularly for best results.   Planting Group 1

526   Bignonia venusta

Bignonia venusta (Pyrostegia venusta)   Zone 10
(Flame Vine)

526   A fast-growing, evergreen vine with brilliant orange, trumpet-shaped flowers that hang in masses during the winter months. Likes the heat of the desert.   Planting Group 1

527   Bignonia violacea

Bignonia violacea (Clytostoma callistegioides)   Zone 9
(Lavender Trumpet Vine)

527   Evergreen. Strong grower, either in sun or shade. Big sprays of 3 in., lavender-violet trumpets on all the tip ends, literally covering the foliage from April to July. Excellent for covering fences, but needs support on a wall.   Planting Group 1

Bougainvillea 'Barbara Karst'   Zone 9

528   Evergreen. Produces more blooms than any other variety. The larger red flower bracts are produced in massive clusters continuously during warm weather. It likes rich soil but plant in full sun and keep on the dry side.   Planting Group 3

528   Bougainvillea 'Barbara Karst'

Bougainvilleas

Only a few of the many varieties—white, pink, red, orange, and many doubles—are found in most nurseries. Be careful when planting. Do not disturb the roots when removing the plant from the container.

532   Bougainvillea 'Manila Red'

529   Bougainvillea 'Brasiliensis'

530   Bougainvillea 'California Gold'

531   Bougainvillea 'Orange King'

Bougainvillea 'Brasiliensis' *(B. spectabilis)*   Zone 9

529   Evergreen. An indescribable mass of color with great clusters of lavender-purple flower bracts. This tropical likes a hot wall with reflected heat. Needs support and dry feet.   Planting Group 3

Bougainvillea 'California Gold'   Zone 9

530   Vigorous evergreen vine with golden yellow "flowers" holding for many months. Do not overwater.   Planting Group 3

Bougainvillea 'Orange King'   Zone 9

531   Attractive sprays of bronzy-orange flowers produced in great abundance during the warm months along with very attractive foliage make this an outstanding plant in warm-weather areas.
Planting Group 3

Bougainvillea 'Manila Red'   Zone 10

532   One of the newer double varieties. This is one of a number of double varieties that have been introduced but are still very scarce in the trade.   Planting Group 3

533   *Bougainvillea* 'San Diego Red'

535   *Campsis tagliabuana* 'Madame Galen'

Bougainvillea 'San Diego Red'   Zone 9
(Scarlett O'Hara)

533   One of the most vigorous of all the *Bougainvilleas.* Deep crimson flowers that do not fade and are borne in large clusters. One of the hardiest.   Planting Group 3

Bougainvillea 'Temple Fire'   Zone 9

534   A low-growing, spreading, bush form with exceptional, fiery red bracts.   Planting Group 3

Cissus antarctica   Zone 9
(Kangaroo Ivy)

536   An evergreen vine, fast-growing, and deep green in color. Widely grown as an indoor plant in the cooler areas and outdoors in warmer areas.   Planting Group 1 or 4

Campsis tagliabuana 'Madame Galen'   Zone 6
(Trumpet Creeper)

535   Deciduous. A vigorous, climbing vine that will cling to most surfaces and produce loose, arching sprays of trumpet-shaped, red flowers. Provides excellent screen. Also grown as a shrub in clump form.   Planting Group 1

534   *Bougainvillea* 'Temple Fire'

536   *Cissus antarctica*

Cissus capensis (Rhoicissus capensis)   Zone 10

(Evergreen Grape)

537   In the warmer areas, a fine, fast-growing, evergreen vine with leaves up to 8 in. Used as a ground cover or fence vine. Sun or shade.

Planting Group 1 or 4

537   Cissus capensis

Cissus rhombifolia   Zone 10

(Grape Ivy)

538   A fast-growing, evergreen vine with glossy foliage. Often used in a hanging basket both indoors and out.   Planting Group 4

538   Cissus rhombifolia

Clematis armandii   Zone 8

539   Evergreen. A spectacular, fast growing vine with beautiful clusters of fragrant, star-like, white flowers that stand out against the dark green background of the foliage. Great on fences, a trellis, or walls. Keep the roots shaded and cool.   Planting Group 4

539   Clematis armandii

CLEMATIS

A large group of vines, mostly deciduous and all having attractive flowers. Some are most spectacular. Best in the northwest or coastal Northern California. It is one plant that should be planted deeper (2 in.) than in the nursery and requires a neutral soil. It also likes a sunny location with roots in the shade.

540A   *Clematis* 'Ernest Markham'

DECIDUOUS VARIETIES

Clematis 'Daniel Deronda'	large, lavender-pink with stripes
Clematis 'Duchess of Edinburgh'	double white
Clematis 'Ernest Markham'	bright cerise-red, light stamens
Clematis 'Gypsy Queen'	deep purple
Clematis henryi	pure white, dark stamens
Clematis jackmanii	deep royal purple
Clematis lanuginosa 'Candida'	large, white, light stamens
Clematis 'Mme. Edouard Andre'	wine-red
Clematis montana rubens	fragrant, rose to pink
Clematis 'Mrs. Cholmondeley'	large, light blue, light stamens
Clematis 'Nelly Moser'	pink and white
Clematis 'Pink Chiffon'	shell-pink, dark stamens
Clematis 'President'	royal purple
Clematis 'Ramona'	light blue

Planting Group 1

540B   *Clematis* 'Mrs. Cholmondeley'

540C   *Clematis* 'Daniel Deronda'

540D   *Clematis lanuginosa* 'Candida'

540E   *Clematis henryi*

540F   *Clematis* 'Nelly Moser'

540G   *Clematis* 'Ernest Markham'

540H   *Clematis* 'Mrs. Cholmondeley'

540I   *Clematis* 'Pink Chiffon'

540J   *Clematis jackmanii*

540K   *Clematis* 'Villa de Lyon'

541   *Fatshedera lizei*

542   *Ficus repens*

543   *Gelsemium sempervirens*

544   *Hedera canariensis*

Fatshedera lizei (Fatsia japonica × Hedera helix)   Zone 8

(Botanical Wonder)

541   Evergreen. A botanical hybrid between *Aralia (Fatsia)* and *Hedera* (Ivy). Has leaves of the *Aralia*. Grows as a small, heavy vine or mounded shrub and is excellent espaliered against a wall. Grows in heavy shade, partial shade, or full sun.   Planting Group 1 or 4

Ficus repens (F. pumila)   Zone 9

(Creeping Fig)

542   Evergreen. One of the few vines that will cling to a masonry wall. Quite vigorous once it starts to climb so wedge it against the wall when planting. Also used indoors as a hanging pot plant.   Planting Group 1

Gelsemium sempervirens   Zone 7

(Carolina Jessamine)

543   Evergreen. Beautiful vine with long, tubular, yellow flowers. These are borne in great abundance from January to April. Best in the warmer regions and in full sun.   Planting Group 1

Hedera canariensis   Zone 8

(Algerian Ivy)

544   Widely used as a bank cover in California and also as a climbing vine to cover a fence. The leaves are large, up to 5 in., and are more tolerant of hot sun than those of most varieties of Ivy. A variegated form also is available.   Planting Group 1

545　Hedera helix

546　Hedera helix 'Hahnsii'

Hedera helix　　　　　　　　　　Zone 4

(English Ivy)

545　One of the hardiest and most widely used of the Ivies. Usually used as a ground cover for banks or as a substitute for a lawn throughout the United States.　　　　　Planting Group 1

547　Hibbertia volubilis

Hedera helix 'Hahnsii'　　　　　　Zone 6

(Hahn's Ivy)

546　Very low-growing variety with small, light green leaves and dense, branching growth. Particularly suited for areas where only a 3 or 4 in. deep cover is wanted. Sun or part shade.
　　　　　Planting Group 1 or 4

Hibbertia volubilis (H. scandens)　　Zone 9

(Guinea Gold Vine)

547　Excellent evergreen vine to 10 ft and especially happy in coastal areas. Shiny dark green leaves and bright yellow, 2½ in., single flowers. Best in partial shade.　　　Planting Group 4

548　Jasminum magnificum

Jasminum magnificum (J. nitidum)　　Zone 10

(Angel Wing Jasmine)

548　A climbing, evergreen shrub or semi-vine with large foliage and glistening, fragrant, white, windmill-like flowers in summer.
　　　　　Planting Group 1

549   *Jasminum polyanthum*

552   *Lonicera japonica 'Halliana'*

550   *Jasminum primulinum*

551   *Longicera hildebrandia*

Jasminum polyanthum   Zone 8
(Pink Jasmine)

549   A vigorous, evergreen climber with lacy foliage. Starting in April it produces masses of pink buds in nice clusters that open to white flowers. Grows in any soil. Fragrant.   Planting Group 1

Jasminum primulinum (J. mesnyi)   Zone 8
(Primrose Jasmine)

550   Evergreen. Fast-growing vine to 10 or 15 ft with bright green leaves and lemon-yellow flowers. Excellent bank cover if you have the room. Planted at 6 ft centers, will grow to 5 or 6 ft then cascade over, making one solid mass of bright green foliage and covered all spring with double yellow flowers.   Planting Group 1

Lonicera hildebrandiana   Zone 9
(Giant Burmese Honeysuckle)

551   A fast-growing, evergreen vine with large, shiny leaves and clusters of giant, 6 in., cream and yellow, fragrant flowers, blooming for more than six months, commencing in late spring.   Planting Group 1

Lonicera japonica 'Halliana'   Zone 5
(Hall's Japanese Honeysuckle or Common Honeysuckle)

552   This vigorous, evergreen vine grows in any soil and is used both as a ground cover and a fence cover. Intensely fragrant, white flowers changing to yellow.   Planting Group 1

Mandevilla 'Alice du Pont'   Zone 9

(Chile Jasmine)

553   Evergreen. Fast growing to 10–15 ft. Dark green leaves to 3 in. with clusters of wide, trumpet-like, intensely fragrant pink flowers. It grows in the sun in rich soil and needs ample water.

Planting Group 1

553   *Mandevilla* 'Alice du Pont'

554   *Passiflora jamesonii*

Passiflora jamesonii   Zone 9

(Jameson or Pink Passion Vine)

554   Evergreen vine with glossy, dark green leaves. It is fast growing and an excellent fence or bank cover. A profuse bloomer all summer with 4 in., tubular flowers that are a lovely, coral-pink color.

Planting Group 1

555   *Passiflora pfordtii*

Passiflora pfordtii (P. alatocaerulea)   Zone 9

(Passion Vine)

555   Large, exotic flowers on this fast-growing, evergreen vine. The fragrant flowers are 3–4 in. across with white petals touched with blue and lavender and a center crown of purple. Flowers all summer.

Planting Group 1

Polygonum aubertii   Zone 4

(Silver Lace Vine)

556   Evergreen to 15°–20°F, then deciduous. Used for a very quick-growing shade or cover. Likes a rich, well-drained soil. Produces masses of fragrant flowers from late spring until fall.

Planting Group 1

556   *Polygonum aubertii*

557   *Rhynchospermum jasminoides*

560   *Solanum jasminoides*

558   *Rosa banksiae* 'Lutea'

559   *Solandra guttata*

Rhynchospermum jasminoides   Zone 7
(Trachelospermum jasminoides)

(Star Jasmine)

557   Evergreen. One of the finest vines for the shade but will do equally well in full sun. Fragrant, white flowers May to July. It is grown as a vine or a mounded shrub and is one of the most beautiful ground covers, but not for a dry bank. This plant likes a peat moss or leaf mold soil with moist roots at all times.   Planting Group 1 or 4

Rosa banksiae 'Lutea'   Zone 6

(Yellow Banksia Rose)

558   Lovely, miniature, double yellow flowers (the size of a good, thick button), borne in clusters on this shiny bright evergreen. Few thorns, if any, and it needs little maintenance. Makes an excellent espalier in the full sun. (*Rosa banksiae* 'Alba' also available. Same characteristics except white in color.)   Planting Group 1

Solandra guttata (S. maxima)   Zone 9

(Cup of Gold Vine)

559   Evergreen, woody vine up to 25 ft. Large, broad, 6 in. leaves, with fragrant, yellow, trumpet flowers having brown stripes. They are fully 8 in. long and 4 in. across. It is one of the fastest growing of all vines. Is salt tolerant at the seashore. Requires full sun.
Planting Group 1

Solanum jasminoides   Zone 9

(Potato Vine)

560   Evergreen to about 28°F, then deciduous. Fast growing to about 15 ft, with small, bright green foliage and white, star-shaped flowers tinged with blue. Needs severe cutting every winter. Sun or partial shade.   Planting Group 1

561   Solanum rantonnetii

562   Stephanotis floribunda

563   Tecoma capensis

568   Wisteria venusta

Solanum rantonnetii   Zone 10

(Blue Solanum or Paraguay Night Shade)

561   Medium to large evergreen vine or shrub. Deep blue flowers from early spring throughout the summer. Must be pruned severely to keep it neat.   Planting Group 1

Stephanotis floribunda   Zone 10

(Madagascar Jasmine)

562   An evergreen vine grown outdoors only in the warmest areas of California but elsewhere as an indoor/outdoor plant. Very fragrant, waxy, funnel-shaped, white flowers. Frequently used in bridal bouquets. When used outdoors, grow in filtered sun with shaded roots.   Planting Group 3

Tecoma capensis (Tecomaria capensis)   Zone 9

(Cape Honeysuckle)

563   Evergreen. A vine or stiff shrub to 15 ft with shiny, dark green foliage and clusters of orange-red, trumpet-shaped flowers. Full sun in well-drained soil. Excellent at the seashore.   Planting Group 1

Wisteria venusta

(Silky Wisteria)

568   Deciduous. Leaves have silky hairs. Individual flowers are very large and open all at once, making a heavy cluster.   Planting Group 1

WISTERIA

All are deciduous, woody vines. Flowers borne in the spring before the leaves. They thrive in deep, rich soil. For ample flowering, fertilize and have even moisture during the summer. Needed pruning should be done in the fall.

All Zone 5

564   *Wisteria floribunda longissima* 'Alba'   pure white flowers from 2–4 ft long.

565   *Wisteria floribunda longissima* 'Rosea'   light pink flowers 2–3 ft long.

566   *Wisteria floribunda longissima* 'Royal Purple'   purple flowers 18 in.–2 ft long.

All Planting Group 1

564   *Wisteria floribunda longissima* 'Alba'

565   *Wisteria floribunda longissima* 'Rosea'

567   *Wisteria sinensis*

Wisteria sinensis (Wisteria chinensis)

(Chinese Wisteria)

567   Deciduous. Most cutting-grown plants in western nurseries are of this type. Flower clusters are about 12 in. and slightly fragrant. Will bloom in considerable shade. Varieties are violet-blue (and usually called purple by nurserymen) and alba.

566   *Wisteria floribunda longissima* 'Royal Purple'

CONIFERS

Abies balsamea 'Nana' Zone 3

(Dwarf Balsam Fir)

569 A very slow-growing, dense, dark green mound, seldom more than 18 in. tall. An interesting bonsai plant for the rock garden in partial shade. Does not like to dry out. Planting Group 1

Abies concolor Zone 3

(White Fir)

570 A native West Coast conifer greatly valued as a Christmas tree and widely grown in western gardens. Makes a very symmetrical tree and it stands pruning. Needles are about 1–1½ in. long and bluish-green in color. Usually a 10 ft tree in 10 years but eventually more than 100 ft. Planting Group 1

570 *Abies concolor*

Abies lasiocarpa Zone 4

(Alpine Fir)

571 Specimens usually 2–4 ft are collected high in the Cascade Mountains, where storms twist them into contorted forms to make them artistic tub plants. Very slow growing. Found mostly in Northwest nurseries. Planting Group 1

569 *Abies balsamea* 'Nana'

571 *Abies lasiocarpa*

572   *Abies pinsapo* 'Glauca'

573   *Araucaria araucana*

Abies pinsapo 'Glauca'   Zone 5
(Blue Spanish Fir)

572   A fine tree with short, stiff, deep bluish-green foliage and dense, symmetrical growth. A native of Spain which will grow in the warm, dry areas to 40 ft. Scarce in the trade.   Planting Group 1

Araucaria araucana   Zone 7
(Monkey Puzzle Tree)

573   This interesting tree has hard, green, stiff, prickly leaves on heavy, spreading branches. Formal in shape, it grows rapidly for the first 10 years, but then slows down as the tree fills out. A 100 ft tree in its native land but seldom more than 50 ft elsewhere.
Planting Group 1

Araucaria bidwillii   Zone 8
(Bunya-Bunya)

574   Bold, symmetrical tree to 60 ft with down-curving limbs covered with sharply pointed, green leaves.   Planting Group 1

574   *Araucaria bidwillii*

575   *Araucaria excelsa*

578   *Cedrus atlantica* 'Glauca Pendula'

576   *Cedrus atlantica*

Araucaria excelsa (A. heterophylla)   Zone 8

(Norfolk Island or Star Pine)

575   Very formal tree usually grown indoors until it gets too big, then planted in the garden where it grows into a beautiful, symmetrical tree to more than 40 ft.   Planting Group 1

Cedrus atlantica   Zone 6

(Atlas Cedar)

576   Large, pyramidal tree with attractive, blue-green, needle-like foliage. Can be used as an excellent bonsai specimen if started early and kept in a tub. This tree will grow to 20 ft in 15 years and eventually to 80 ft.   Planting Group 1

Cedrus atlantica 'Glauca'   Zone 6

(Blue Atlas Cedar)

577   Grafted plants ensure the bright blue foliage of this plant, which is considered the most beautiful of the blue Conifers. Grows in a natural bonsai style.   Planting Group 1

Cedrus atlantica 'Glauca Pendula'   Zone 6

578   This beautiful, weeping form of *C. a.* 'Glauca' can be trained to any shape. The branches droop vertically and, with age, it makes a superb specimen. Crawls along the ground unless staked.
                    Planting Group 1

577   *Cedrus atlantica* 'Glauca'

579   Cedrus deodara

581   Cedrus deodara 'Prostrata'

Cedrus deodara 'Aurea'   Zone 7

580   This grafted plant is not so fast growing nor does it grow so big as *C. deodara*. This variety has golden yellow foliage turning to yellowish-green in the fall. Seldom more than 20 ft.
                                                            Planting Group 1

Cedrus deodara   Zone 7

(California Christmas Tree)

579   Rich, silver gray-green on this fast-growing tree that has wide, spreading branches, needle-like leaves, and drooping tip. It is best in the interior valley where it grows to 100 ft or more but not too good along the coast.   Planting Group 1

Cedrus deodara 'Prostrata'   Zone 7

(Weeping Deodar)

581   This variety will grow flat on the ground or even hang over a wall. Stands pruning. Very scarce in the trade.   Planting Group 1

Cedrus libani   Zone 5

(Cedar of Lebanon)

582   Large evergreen to 100 ft with short, blue-green needles. Each tree will vary in shape and foliage color. Train to desired shape. Slow growing. Scarce in the trade.   Planting Group 1

580   Cedrus deodara 'Aurea'

582   Cedrus libani

583   *Chamaecyparis lawsoniana*

584   *Chamaecyparis lawsoniana* 'Allumii'

Chamaecyparis lawsoniana   Zone 5
(Port Orford Cedar or Lawson Cypress)

583   Important timber tree in coastal Oregon and Northern California. It grows in a pyramidal form to 100 ft or more. Many varieties in
the trade today trace their origins to this variety.   Planting Group 1

Chamaecyparis lawsoniana 'Allumii'   Zone 5
(Blue Lawson Cypress)

584   Compact, narrow, pyramidal tree to 30 ft with flat, metallic-blue
foliage. Best in the interior where the drainage is good with only
limited amounts of water.   Planting Group 2

Chamaecyparis lawsoniana 'Nidiformis'   Zone 6
(Birdnest Cypress)

586   The natural habit of this plant is wider than tall; seldom reaching a height of more than 4 ft. An excellent, dark green, low-growing
foundation plant for a hot, sunny location. Needs good drainage.
                                                         Planting Group 2

Chamaecyparis lawsoniana 'Ellwoodii'   Zone 5
(Ellwood Cypress)

585   A moderate to slow grower of columnar type to 10 ft. Foliage is
silver-blue, soft, and lacy. The tree is neat and attractive but must be
planted where the drainage is excellent as it, like most Cypresses, is
extremely sensitive to wet feet.   Planting Group 2

586   *Chamaecyparis lawsoniana* 'Nidiformis'

585   *Chamaecyparis lawsoniana* 'Ellwoodii'

588 *Chamaecyparis obtusa* 'Aurea'

587 *Chamaecyparis obtusa*

Chamaecyparis obtusa   Zone 5
(Hinoki Cypress)

587   This most artistic tree is slow growing and most gardeners treat it as a dwarf even though it will grow to a small tree up to 15 and even 50 ft in 50 years. Generally pyramidal in habit, it is best when trained to emphasize its irregular branching. Needs good drainage and is best in the Northern California, Oregon, and Washington coastal areas in full sun; is not too happy in the hot interior.   Planting Group 2

Chamaecyparis obtusa 'Aurea'   Zone 6
(Golden Hinoki Cypress)

588   Similar to *C. obtusa* but slower growing. Even in the cooler coastal regions, this plant is best with morning sun only as the foliage burns rather easily. Needs good drainage.
                              Planting Group 2

Chamaecyparis obtusa 'Crippsii'   Zone 6
(Cripps Golden Cypress)

589   Pyramidal in form, but a more open habit of growth than most *C. obtusas*. One of the most beautiful specimen trees in the 15 or 20 ft range. Best in the cooler coastal areas of Northern California and farther north.   Planting Group 2

589 *Chamaecyparis obtusa* 'Crippsii'

590 *Chamaecyparis obtusa* 'Minima'

593 *Chamaecyparis pisifera* 'Cyano Viridis'

591 *Chamaecyparis obtusa* 'Nana'

Chamaecyparis obtusa 'Minima' Zone 7

590 A soft-textured, compact, globular plant seldom more than a foot tall but up to 3 ft broad. Excellent rock garden or pot plant.

Planting Group 1

Chamaecyparis obtusa 'Nana' Zone 5
(Dwarf Hinoki Cypress)

591 Low, globular plant with deep green foliage. It is rated as one of the choicest plants in the garden. Excellent tub plant; very slow growing, and needs good drainage. It must be protected from dogs. Best in the cooler coastal regions. Planting Group 2

Chamaecyparis obtusa 'Torulosa' Zone 5

592 This plant is different. Dark green, twisted, threadlike branches with scalelike leaves which give this plant a natural bonsai look. It will grow to 6 ft but, with a little bonsai pruning, it is easily kept to 3 ft. Excellent pot or rock garden plant. Planting Group 2

Chamaecyparis pisifera 'Cyano Viridis' Zone 4
(Blue Plume Cypress)

593 A graceful pyramidal tree to 10 ft, sometimes more, with soft plumelike, sivery-blue foliage that forms an irregular rounded cone-shaped tree. One of the few "blue" plants that will tolerate the shade.

Planting Group 4

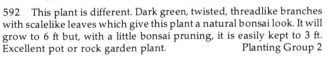

592 *Chamaecyparis obtusa* 'Torulosa'

595 *Chamaecyparis pisifera* 'Plumosa'

594 *Chamaecyparis pisifera* 'Filifera' and *C.p.* 'Filifera Aurea'

Chamaecyparis pisifera 'Filifera' Zone 3
(Threadbranch Cypress)

594 While this plant will eventually make a small tree, it is usually planted as a large shrub, and, with minimum amounts of pruning, can be kept within bounds. If thinned, it has an Oriental look that is hard to beat. Planting Group 2

Chamaecyparis pisifera 'Plumosa' Zone 5
(Plume Cypress)

595 A very nice, conical, small tree with dark green foliage and short needles. While it eventually will grow to 20 ft, it is quite slow to 8 or 10 ft and is a good, small, garden evergreen. Planting Group 2

Chamaecyparis pisifera 'Filifera Aurea' Zone 3
(Golden Threadleaf Cypress)

594 This slightly golden threadleaf variety is not so upright as the green form. The branches are flattened, threadleaf, and slightly drooping. Very attractive. Planting Group 2

Cryptomeria japonica 'Elegans' Zone 5
(Plume Cryptomeria)

596 Feathery, gray-green, soft-textured foliage that turns purplish or coppery-red in winter. An outstanding pyramid to 25 ft or more. Planting Group 1

Cryptomeria japonica 'Elegans Nana' Zone 6

597 A compact, pyramidal, dwarf form with bright foliage turning to plum-red in the fall. Planting Group 4

596 *Cryptomeria japonica* 'Elegans'

597 *Cryptomeria japonica* 'Elegans Nana'

598   Cupressocyparis leylandii

Cupressocyparis leylandii   Zone 5
(Leyland Cypress)

598   A rapid-growing, narrow pyramid to 30 ft with striking green, dense foliage. Excellent, tall hedge plant or windbreak. Needs pruning when young and accepts a wide variety of soils and climates.
                                                          Planting Group 1

599   Cupressus glabra

Cupressus glabra (C. arizonica)   Zone 6
(Arizona Cypress)

599   A tall, upright Conifer to 20 ft with grayish-green foliage. Its ability to stand heat and drought in the Southwest makes this tree a favorite in hot-weather country.
                                       Planting Group 1

Cupressus macrocarpa   Zone 7
(Monterey Cypress)

600   A good seashore plant. Beautiful, dark green tree to 40 ft becoming picturesquely irregular when exposed to wind or sea. Often used as a seashore windbreak or tall hedge.   Planting Group 1

Cupressus sempervirens 'Glauca'   Zone 7
(Italian Cypress)

601   Narrow, dense, columnar tree with silver-blue-green foliage. Often 20 ft tall and only 2 ft in diameter. A fine accent plant for the landscape.   Planting Group 1

601   Cupressus sempervirens 'Glauca'

600   Cupressus macrocarpa

602   *Juniperus chinensis* 'Armstrongii'

603   *Juniperus chinensis* 'Armstrongii Coasti'

605   *Juniperus chinensis* 'Blue Point'

Juniperus chinensis 'Armstrongii'   Zone 4
(Armstrong Juniper)

602   Lacy, light green foliage on this compact, medium-sized, nestlike Juniper. Its closely knit habit of growth makes this an excellent garden addition.   Planting Group 1

Juniperus chinensis 'Armstrongii Coasti'   Zone 4
(Coasti Juniper)

603   Outstanding golden coloring on this dense compact plant. Very little trimming is necessary and the gold holds even in cold weather.
                    Planting Group 1

Juniperus chinensis 'Blaauw'   Zone 5
(Blaauw's Juniper)

604   An upright, vase-shaped Juniper to about 4 ft with dark blue foliage on this neat, compact plant.   Planting Group 1

Juniperus chinensis 'Blue Point'   Zone 5
(Blue Point Juniper)

605   A very formal appearance, dense, pyramidal form, and beautiful, blue-gray foliage make this a very excellent plant. Also sought after because of its tolerance to extremes of heat and poor soil.
                    Planting Group 1

604   *Juniperus chinensis* 'Blaauw'

606 *Juniperus chinensis* 'Hetzi Glauca'

607 *Juniperus chinensis* 'Pfitzerana'

Juniperus chinensis 'Hetzi Glauca' Zone 3

(Hetzi Blue Juniper)

606 Semi-erect Juniper with a light frosty blue foliage. It is fast growing with a medium-large spread. Planting Group 1

Juniperus chinensis 'Pfitzerana' Zone 3

(Pfitzer Juniper)

607 A fast-growing, spreading shrub with rich gray-green, feathery foliage. Grows 3–4 ft high and 6–8 ft across. Can be kept in bounds by heavy pruning. Used as a low accent plant or as a ground cover. Planting Group 1

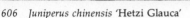

608 *Juniperus chinensis* 'Pfitzerana Aurea'

Juniperus chinensis 'Pfitzerana Aurea' Zone 4

(Golden Pfitzer Juniper)

608 Beautiful, gray-greenish foliage tipped with gold throughout the year. Grows to 4 or 5 ft tall and about 8 ft across. Planting Group 1

Juniperus chinensis 'Pfitzerana Glauca' Zone 4

(Blue Pfitzer Juniper)

609 Soft silver-blue foliage and a spreading, compact habit of growth. Mature plants may reach 6–8 ft in height with a 10–15 ft spread. Planting Group 1

609 *Juniperus chinensis* 'Pfitzerana Glauca'

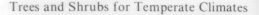

610   *Juniperus chinensis* 'Procumbens'

611   *Juniperus chinensis* 'Procumbens Nana'

612   *Juniperus chinensis* 'Robust Green'

613   *Juniperus chinensis* 'San Jose'

Juniperus chinensis 'Procumbens'   Zone 4
(Japanese Garden Juniper)

610   A very flat, wide-spreading (to 6 ft) variety with sharply pointed, bluish-green foliage. Excellent around rock work and widely used by the Japanese in their gardens.   Planting Group 1

Juniperus chinensis 'Procumbens Nana'   Zone 4

611   Extremely compact, low-spreading Juniper with dense, blue-green foliage. Excellent bonsai material. One of the best varieties of the low-creeping evergreens. Spectacular when grown "staked" in a container and shaped.   Planting Group 1

Juniperus chinensis 'Robust Green'   Zone 5

612   Informal, irregular, upright growth with bright green foliage. A most outstanding Juniper but fairly slow growing.   Planting Group 1

Juniperus chinensis 'San Jose'   Zone 4
(San Jose Juniper)

613   An excellent, semi-prostrate Juniper with sage-green, compact foliage. One of the best Junipers for bonsai use. Good tub plant.
                                                      Planting Group 1

615 Juniperus chinensis 'Torulosa'

614 Juniperus chinensis 'Sea Green'

Juniperus chinensis 'Sea Green'   Zone 5

(Sea Green Juniper)

614 An oustanding spreading Juniper with deep green coloring. It has a compact habit and arching branches. Very similar growth to *J. c.* 'Pfitzerana'; does not grow so fast, but will grow taller.   Planting Group 1

Juniperus chinensis 'Torulosa' (*J. c.* 'Kaizuka')   Zone 5

(Hollywood Juniper)

615 Artistic, dense, upright-growing Juniper. Twisted branches and rich dark green foliage. Should be planted away from the house where it has enough room to twist and turn, performing the way it should.
                                                        Planting Group 1

Juniperus communis 'Stricta'   Zone 4

(Irish Juniper)

616 Fast growing. Very narrow column with gray-green foliage. Many similar plants are sold under other names, e.g., *J. c. fastigiata* and *J. c.hibernica*.   Planting Group 1

Juniperus conferta 'Blue Pacific'   Zone 6

(Shore Juniper)

617 Improved form of *J. conferta.* A low-creeping form, seldom more than 6 in. tall. Excellent around rock work or hanging over a wall. Best in the cooler coastal areas as this one does not like full sun in the hot interior.   Planting Group 1

616 Juniperus communis 'Stricta'

617 Juniperus conferta 'Blue Pacific'

618   Juniperus horizontalis

Juniperus horizontalis 'Bar Harbor'   Zone 4

(Bar Harbor Juniper)

619   One of the best of the very prostrate Junipers because, as it grows, its branches hug the ground. Summer foliage is soft gray-blue turning to silvery plum color in winter.   Planting Group 1

619   Juniperus horizontalis 'Bar Harbor'

620   Juniperus horizontalis 'Variegata'

Juniperus horizontalis   Zone 4

618   Prostrate, creeping to form a low, flat, compact mat with stiff, bluish-green foliage that makes interesting patterns.
                                  Planting Group 1

621   Juniperus horizontalis 'Wiltonii'

Juniperus horizontalis 'Variegata'   Zone 4

620   This low-growing, flat, spreading Juniper has bluish-green foliage liberally splashed with blotches of creamy variegation. Variegation will burn in very hot sun.   Planting Group 1

Juniperus horizontalis 'Wiltonii'   Zone 4

(Blue Carpet Juniper)

621   This living carpet is similar in habit to 'Bar Harbor' and one of the finest low-trailing Junipers. Foliage is intense silver-blue.
                                  Planting Group 1

Juniperus sabina 'Arcadia'   Zone 3

(Arcadia Juniper)

622   Bright green foliage with a lacy texture on this attractive, low-growing evergreen. Fine mass border or foundation plant.
                                  Planting Group 1

Juniperus sabina 'Broadmoor'   Zone 3

623   A fairly new introduction with attractive green foliage. Grows to about 1 ft. Will take full sun but also is happy with coastal conditions.
                                  Planting Group 1

622   *Juniperus sabina* 'Arcadia'

623   *Juniperus sabina* 'Broadmoor'

Juniperus sabina 'Buffalo'   Zone 3

624   A new, bright green, wide-spreading, low-growing form of Juniper with soft, feathery branches. Very hardy and excellent in coastal areas as well as colder areas.   Planting Group 1

Juniperus sabina 'Tamariscifolia'   Zone 3

(Tamarix Juniper or Tam Juniper)

625   Spreads close to the ground, making a solid mat, seldom more than 18 in. in mature plants. Foliage is bright blue-green. Excellent ground cover.   Planting Group 1

624   *Juniperus sabina* 'Buffalo'

Juniperus scopulorum 'Blue Heaven'   Zone 4

(Blue Heaven Juniper)

626   A very compact, pyramidal form to about 12 ft. It is one of the bluest of all the Junipers and makes an excellent accent plant where color contrast is needed. Needs full sun.   Planting Group 1

626   *Juniperus scopulorum* 'Blue Heaven'

625   *Juniperus sabina* 'Tamariscifolia'

627   Juniperus scopulorum 'Pathfinder'

628   Juniperus squamata 'Meyeri'

Juniperus squamata 'Meyeri'   Zone 5
(Meyer Juniper)

628   This is an oddly shaped, blue-green, rather stiff Juniper which grows to 6 or 8 ft tall with about the same spread.   Planting Group 1

Juniperus scopulorum 'Pathfinder' Zone 3
(Pathfinder Juniper)

627   A showy, dense, broad, pyramidal Juniper with a bright blue-gray cast to the foliage. Full sun and a dry location.
Planting Group 1

Juniperus virginiana 'Silver Spreader'   Zone 4
(Silver Spreader Juniper)

629   A very delightful, spreading Conifer with shiny, silvery foliage. Excellent ground cover.   Planting Group 1

Libocedrus decurrens (Calocedrus decurrens)   Zone 5
(Incense Cedar)

630   A very symmetrical, narrow, columnar tree to 100 ft with deep green, fragrant foliage. A California native.   Planting Group 1

630   Libocedrus decurrens

629   Juniperus virginiana 'Silver Spreader'

633 *Picea excelsa* 'Nidiformis'

631 *Metasequoia glypostroboides*

Metasequoia glyptostroboides   Zone 5

(Dawn Redwood)

631 Deciduous. A beautiful, rapid-growing Conifer, resembling the California coastal Redwood. The foliage is bright green and very soft to the touch. Grows best in soil with lots of humus and generous amounts of water.   Planting Group 1

Picea excelsa 'Nidiformis' (*P. abies* 'Nidiformis')   Zone 4

(Nest Spruce)

633 Low, rounded, nestlike shrub that grows 2–4 in. a year to about 18 in., and 5–6 ft across. Needles are very short and fine. New foliage bright green. Best in cooler areas.   Planting Group 1

Picea excelsa (*P. abies*)   Zone 2

(Norway Spruce)

632 Widely sold as a living Christmas tree. This tree does quite well in cooler areas. Needs pruning to keep it compact.   Planting Group 1

Picea excelsa 'Pendula' (*P. abies* 'Pendula')   Zone 3

(Weeping Norway Spruce)

634 The dense, rich green foliage on the branches and branchlets of this interesting specimen makes it a favorite. A natural bonsai type plant that grows best in Northern California along the coast and in the Northwest.   Planting Group 1

634 *Picea excelsa* 'Pendula'

632 *Picea excelsa*

635   *Picea excelsa* 'Pygmaea'

637   *Picea pungens*

Picea excelsa 'Pygmaea'   Zone 6
(*P. abies* 'Pygmaea')

635   Stiff, deep green, attractive needles on
this very slow-growing evergreen Conifer. In
20 years this one could be only 2–3 ft tall and 2
ft broad. For a rock garden or a tub plant this
one is excellent. Needs well-drained, moist
soil.   Planting Group 1

Picea glauca 'Conica'   Zone 3
(Dwarf Alberta Spruce)

636   A miniature tree that maintains a perfect conical shape and
grows only about 6 in. a year with very short needles, bright green
when new, then gray-green. Excellent tub plant and miniature Christmas tree for years.   Planting Group 1

Picea pungens   Zone 3
(Colorado Spruce)

637   A broad, pyramidal Spruce with horizontal and stiff, sharp,
green needle foliage. All are seedling grown and usually 50% will be
green, 35% blue-green, and 15% blue. The blue and blue-green com-
mand a premium price.   Planting Group 2

Picea pungens 'Koster'   Zone 3
(Koster Blue Spruce)

638   Grafted plants only. These have a richer blue form and longer
needles. Very erratic grower in early stages. Shaping will help attain
"Christmas tree" look.   Planting Group 2

636   *Picea glauca* 'Conica'

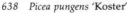

638   *Picea pungens* 'Koster'

641   *Pinus canariensis*

639   *Picea pungens* 'Moerheimii'

Picea pungens 'Moerheimii'   Zone 3
(Moerheim Spruce)

639   Grafts only. Similar to the 'Koster' variety but more compact and grows straighter.   Planting Group 2

Pinus aristata   Zone 1
(Bristlecone Pine)

640   A beautiful, extremely hardy Conifer. Will stand temperatures from 100° to −50°. Very slow-growing, artistic tub plant or bonsai for a long period of time. Good drainage necessary.   Planting Group 1

Pinus canariensis   Zone 8
(Canary Island Pine)

641   One of the most beautiful Pines grown in warmer climates. While considered an "ugly duckling" in a container, it grows to 100 ft straight, symmetrical tree with horizontal branches, evenly spaced in whorls. The long needles are thickly placed in large tufts. Somewhat tender in the colder areas.   Planting Group 1

Pinus densiflora 'Umbraculifera'   Zone 4
(Table Mountain Pine or Tanyosho Pine)

642   Excellent container or rock garden plant usually growing wider than it does tall. Grafted plants only. It can take 20 years to get to be 6 ft tall and as wide.   Planting Group 1

642   *Pinus densiflora* 'Umbraculifera'

640   *Pinus aristata*

643   *Pinus halepensis*

Pinus halepensis   Zone 7
(Aleppo Pine)

643   A round-headed, irregularly shaped Pine
to 40 ft with short, gray-green needles. This
Pine thrives on neglect and is best when
planted in a very dry location. Also good near
the seashore.   Planting Group 1

644   *Pinus mugo*

Pinus mugo   Zone 2
(Mugho Pine)

644   One of the smallest of all the Pines in the trade, growing about as
wide as it does tall. Widely used in rock gardens; also an excellent low
foundation or container plant. Very slow grower; likes a dry location
best. Stands pruning.   Planting Group 1

Pinus nigra   Zone 3
(Austrian Black Pine)

645   A large, densely foliaged pyramid Pine with dark, shiny foliage.
Grows to about 40 ft.   Planting Group 1

Pinus patula   Zone 8
(Jelecote Pine)

646   A very graceful and unusual Pine growing to about 40 ft. A
beautiful, irregular tree with long, yellow-green, silky needles that
hang down, giving it a "different" look with its lacy appearance.
                 Planting Group 2

645   *Pinus nigra*

646   *Pinus patula*

647 *Pinus pinea*

Pinus pinea   Zone 7

(Italian Stone Pine)

647 Native to the Mediterranean, where it will stand heat and drought but is not hurt by generous garden watering. Never attractive as a nursery sized tree, but after 10 years its picturesque spreading beauty is evident and greatly enjoyed.   Planting Group 1

Pinus radiata   Zone 8

(Monterey Pine)

648 A widely planted Pine tree around the world. Grows rapidly and succeeds anywhere. Used as a windbreak or an individual specimen. Deep green foliage. Tall and symmetrical to 20 ft in 10 years, 75 ft or more eventually.   Planting Group 1

Pinus strobus 'Nana'   Zone 4

649 This five-needle Pine is the dwarf form of *P. strobus*, which is native to northwestern United States. It has very soft foliage and a nice, rounded shape. However, it does not like to dry out and does not like the wind. Excellent rock garden or tub plant. Found mostly in North-west nurseries.   Planting Group 1

648 *Pinus radiata*

Pinus sylvestris   Zone 4

(Scotch Pine)

650 When young, this Pine is straight, well-branched, and pyramidal, but as it grows it becomes irregular and picturesque. Grows to 80 ft. Good almost anywhere from coast to coast except in the desert.   Planting Group 1

649 *Pinus strobus* 'Nana'

650 *Pinus sylvestris*

651   *Pinus sylvestris* 'Fastigiata'

654   *Podocarpus gracilior*

652   *Pinus thunbergiana*

Pinus sylvestris 'Fastigiata'   Zone 4

651   Similar foliage and growing conditions as the parent but the
branches of this cultivar grow straight and next to the trunk. When the
tree is 10 ft tall it is seldom more than 3 ft in diameter.

Planting Group 1

Pinus thunbergiana   Zone 5

(Japanese Black Pine)

652–653   Irregular pattern of pyramidal growth, blackish-gray bark,
and sharp, green needles. Decorative in planters when young and kept
pruned and shaped. Two pictures have been used, one trained as a
bonsai, the other allowed to grow. Both are about the same age.

Planting Group 1

653   *Pinus thunbergiana*

655   *Podocarpus macrophyllus*

656　Podocarpus macrophyllus maki

657　Pseudotsuga taxifolia

Podocarpus gracilior   Zone 9

(Fern Pine)

654　A plant of compact growth similar to *P. elongatus,* but this has a heavier trunk and does not drop its lower branches. The foliage is much denser. Excellent tub plant both indoors and outdoors and in the garden used as a heavily-trimmed shrub, small tree, or espalier. Few people realize this plant is a Conifer.   Planting Group 1

Podocarpus macrophyllus   Zone 7

(Yew Podocarpus)

655　Evergreen shrub or small tree to 15 ft with Yew-like, deep rich green foliage. Usually kept trimmed like a Yew to a columnar form. Excellent indoor plant.   Planting Group 1 or 4

Podocarpus macrophyllus maki   Zone 7

(Shrubby Yew Pine)

656　Similar to *P. macrophyllus* but the plant is more compact, more erect, and the needles are much shorter. Likes to be pruned to shape.   Planting Group 1 or 4

Sciadopitys verticillata   Zone 4

(Umbrella Pine)

658　Evergreen Conifer to about 25 ft on the West Coast, but to 100 ft in native Japan. Young plants are symmetrical and rather narrow. The dark green needles are 3–6 in. long and in whorls. The plants should never be allowed to dry out and require a rich, well-drained soil. Ecellent tub specimen or in the ground. Can take full sun (or shade) near the coast; requires a rich, well-drained soil and should have afternoon shade in the hot interior.   Planting Group 2

Pseudotsuga taxifolia (P. menziesii)   Zone 5

(Douglas Fir)

657　Native to the Pacific Coast from California north and much prized as a Christmas tree. Sharply pyramidal form when young growing eventually to 200 ft; soft, fragrant foliage.   Planting Group 1

658　Sciadopitys verticillata

659 *Sequoia gigantea*

660 *Sequoia gigantea* 'Pendulum'

Sequoia gigantea (Sequoiadendron giganteum)   Zone 6
(Giant Sequoia)

659 The giant Redwood has a conical shape with a dense, branching habit and blue-green foliage. It grows too fast and is usually too big for the average garden.   Planting Group 1

Sequoia sempervirens   Zone 7
(Coast Redwood)

661 A fast-growing, conical tree, with dark green, flat, needle-like leaves; usually too big for a city garden. Best with regular watering.
                                                          Planting Group 1

Sequoia gigantea 'Pendulum'   Zone 6
(Sequoiadendron giganteum 'Pendulum')
(Weeping Giant Sequoia)

660 A weeping form of the giant "Big Tree" and for the first few years seldom has branches more than 2 ft long. It has a very interesting shape and is very scarce in the trade, mostly in the Northwest. Must be placed carefully in the garden for best display.   Planting Group 1

661 *Sequoia sempervirens*

662 *Taxus baccata*

663 *Taxus baccata* 'Fastigiata'

Taxus baccata 'Repandens Aurea'   Zone 6

(Golden Spreading Yew)

666 Long, golden branches; seldom more than 2 ft tall but spreading a great deal more. Excellent rock garden or low foundation plant but needs good drainage.   Planting Group 2

664 *Taxus baccata* 'Fastigiata Aurea'

666 *Taxus baccata* 'Repandens Aurea'

Taxus baccata   Zone 6

(English Yew)

662 As gardens become smaller and smaller, this tree is fast decreasing in popularity as it needs a great deal of room. It is listed in this book only because so many people ask for it by the common name when they are actually asking for the tight, upright, pyramidal form, *T. b.* 'Fastigiata', the Irish Yew. The English Yew spreads as wide as it grows tall, up to 30 ft.   Planting Group 2

Taxus baccata 'Fastigiata'   Zone 6

(Irish Yew)

663 Formal, slender column of the deepest green foliage. Ideal accent plant beside doors or in a corner. Slow, upright growth. Will not stand poorly drained soil.   Planting Group 2

Taxus baccata 'Fastigiata Aurea'   Zone 6

664 Same as *T. b.* 'Fastigiata', except with golden tips and margins.
Planting Group 1

Taxus baccata 'Repandens'   Zone 5

(Spreading English Yew)

665 A very useful, spreading plant, seldom more than 2 ft tall; ideal for foundation planting as well as hanging over a wall.
Planting Group 2

665 *Taxus baccata* 'Repandens'

668   *Thuja occidentalis* 'Pyramidalis'

667   *Thuja occidentalis* 'Little Gem'

Thuja occidentalis 'Pyramidalis'   Zone 2
(Pyramidal Arborvitae)

668   A beautiful accent plant. Slow growing, very slender, compact plant with soft, dark-green, fan-shaped foliage. A large plant in southern latitudes 9–10 ft tall; however, it grows taller in the Northwest as a perfect pyramid without trimming. Sun or shade.
                                                    Planting Group 1

Thuja occidentalis 'Little Gem'   Zone 2
(Green Globe Arborvitae)

667   Dark green foliage with short, dense, green growth to about 3 ft. Very slow.
                                    Planting Group 1

Thuja occidentalis 'Woodwardii'   Zone 2

669   Widely grown, dense, globular *Thuja* with rich green foliage. Usually a nice tree to 5 ft, but with age can get too large. Maintains its shape without pruning.   Planting Group 1

Thuja orientalis 'Aurea Nana'   Zone 6
(*Platycladus orientalis* 'Aureus Nanus')
(Dwarf Golden Arborvitae)

670   Most popular dwarf Arborvitae, seldom more than 4 ft. Slow-growing, dense, pointed globe with golden-yellow branches year around. Hardy to heat, cold, and dry conditions, and best kept out of range of dogs.   Planting Group 1

670   *Thuja orientalis* 'Aurea Nana'

669   *Thuja occidentalis* 'Woodwardii'

671   *Thuja orientalis* 'Beverleyensis'

672   *Tsuga canadensis*

Thuja orientalis 'Beverleyensis'   Zone 5
(*Platycladus orientalis* 'Beverleyensis'
(Beverly Hills Arborvitae)

671   Bright golden foliage on this narrow specimen. At 12 ft is usually
4 or 5 ft wide. Requires full sun to maintain its golden color.
                                         Planting Group 1

Tsuga canadensis   Zone 3
(Canadian Hemlock)

672   Grows to a large, pyramidal tree with horizontal branches which
have pendulous tips. Widely grown as a dense hedge in the Northwest. For this type, prune when young.   Planting Group 1

Tsuga canadensis 'Pendula'   Zone 4
(Sargent Weeping Hemlock)

673   A weeping form of the Canadian Hemlock. Grows broader than
it does high, forming a rounded dome with the pendulous branches
reaching to the ground or over a wall.   Planting Group 1

673   *Tsuga canadensis* 'Pendula'

List of Common to Botanic Names

COMMON	BOTANIC
Aaron's Beard	*Hypericum calycinum*
African Boxwood	*Myrsine africana*
Aleppo Pine	*Pinus halepensis*
Alpine Fir	*Abies lasiocarpa*
Angel's Trumpet	*Datura suaveolens*
Angel Wing Jasmine	*Jasminum magnificum*
Arborvitae	*Thuja*
Arizona Cypress	*Cupressus glabra*
Atlas Cedar	*Cedrus atlantica*
Australian Bluebell Creeper	*Sollya heterophylla*
Australian Fuchsia	*Correa pulchella*
Australian Tea Tree	*Leptospernum laevigatum*
Australian Tree Fern	*Alsophila australis*
Australian Black Pine	*Pinus nigra*
Baby's Breath	*Diosma erioides*
Bailey Acacia	*Acacia baileyana*
Bamboo	*Bambusa*
Banana Shrub	*Michelia fuscata*
Banana Tree	*Musa ensete*
Barberry	*Berberis*
Banksia Rose	*Rosa banksiae*
Bearberry Cotoneaster	*Cotoneaster dammeri*
Bear's Breech	*Acanthus mollis*
Beauty Bush	*Kolkwitzia*
Bird of Paradise	*Strelitzia reginae*
Bird of Paradise Shrub	*Poinciana gilliesii*
Bird of Paradise Tree	*Strelitzia nicolai*
Birdnest Cypress	*Chamaecyparis lawsoniana* 'Nidiformis'
Blackwood Acacia	*Acacia melanoxylon*
Blue Atlas Cedar	*Cedrus atlantica* 'Glauca'
Blue Cocos Palm	*Cocos australis*
Blue Leadwort	*Ceratostigma plumbaginoides*
Blue Spanish Fir	*Abies pinsapo glauca*
Bog Rosemary	*Andromeda polifolia*
Boston Ivy	*Ampelopsis tricuspidata*
Boston Sword Fern	*Nephrolepis exaltata*
Botanical Wonder	*Fatshedera lizei*
Bottlebrush	*Callistemon*
Bottle Ponytail	*Beaucarnea recurvata*
Bottle Tree	*Sterculia diversifolia*
Box Leaf Azara	*Azara microphylla*
Boxwood	*Buxus*
Brazilian Flame Bush	*Calliandra tweedii*
Bridal Wreath	*Spiraea vanhouttei*
Bradford Pear	*Pyrus calleryana bradford*
Brisbane Box	*Tristania*
Bristlecone Pine	*Pinus aristata*
Brazilian Pepper	*Schinus terebinthifolius*
Brush Cherry	*Eugenua myrtifolia*
Buckwheat	*Eriogonum arborescens*
Bunya-Bunya	*Araucaria bidwillii*
Burford Holly	*Ilex cornuta burfordii*

Bush Anenome	*Carpenteria californica*
Bush Morning Glory	*Convolvulus cneorum*
Bushy Yate	*Eucalyptus lehmannii*
Butterfly Iris	*Moraea iridioides*
California Christmas Tree	*Cedrus deodara*
California Fan Palm	*Washingtonia filifera*
California Pepper Tree	*Schinus molle*
California Privet	*Ligustrum ovalifolium*
Camphor Tree	*Camphora officinarum*
Canary Bird Bush	*Crotalaria agatiflora*
Canary Island Pine	*Pinus canariensis*
Canoe Birch	*Betula papyrifera*
Cape Honeysuckle	*Tecoma capensis*
Cape Plumbago	*Plumbago capensis*
Carob	*Ceratonia siliqua*
Carolina Cherry	*Prunus caroliniana*
Carolina Jessamine	*Gelsemium sempervirens*
Carrot Wood	*Cupaniopsis anacardioides*
Cast Iron Plant	*Aspidistra elatior*
Catalina Cherry	*Prunus integrifolia lyonii*
Catalina Ironwood	*Lyonothamnus*
Cat's Claw	*Bignonia chamberlaynii*
Cedar	*Cedrus*
Cedar of Lebanon	*Cedrus libani*
Chile Jasmine	*Mandevilla suaveolens*
Chilian Guava	*Myrtus ugni*
Chinese Flame Tree	*Koelreuteria bipinnata*
Chinese Hollygrape	*Mahonia lomariifolia*
Cinquefoil	*Potentilla*
Coast Live Oak	*Quercus agrifolia*
Coast Redwood	*Sequoia sempervirens*
Colorado Spruce	*Picea pungens*
Copper Beech	*Fagus sylvatica purpurea*
Coral Bark Maple	*Acer palmatum* 'Sangokaku'
Coral Gum	*Eucalyptus torquata*
Cork Oak	*Quercus suber*
Crape Myrtle	*Lagerstroemia*
Crimson King Maple	*Acer platanoides* 'Crimson King'
Creeping Fig	*Ficus repens*
Cup of Gold Vine	*Solandra guttata*
Currant	*Ribes*
Cutleaf Weeping Birch	*Betula alba laciniata*
Cycad	*Cycas*
Cypress	*Chamaecyparis or cupressocyparis or cupressus*
Darwin Barberry	*Berberis darwinii*
Date Palm	*Phoenix canariensis*
Dawn Redwood	*Metasequoia glyptostroboides*
Dwarf Alberta Spruce	*Picea glauca* 'Conica'
Dwarf Natal Plum	*Carissa grandiflora prostrata*
Desert Gum	*Eucalyptus rudis*
Desert Willow Pittosporum	*Pittosporum phillyraeoides*
Diamond Leaf Pittosporum	*Pittosporum rhombifolium*
Dogwood	*Cornus*
Douglas Fir	*Pseudotsuga taxifolia*
Dracena Palm	*Cordyline indivisa*
Dusty Miller	*Centaurea cineraria*
Dwarf Balsam Fir	*Abies balsamea* 'Nana'
Dwarf Blue Gum	*Eucalyptus globulus compacta*
Easter Lily Vine	*Beaumontia grandiflora*
Egyptian Paper Reed	*Cyperus papyrus*
Elm	*Ulmus*
English Laurel	*Prunus laurocerasus*
English Yew	*Taxus baccata*

European Hornbeam	*Carpinus betulus 'Columnaris'*
Evergreen Grape	*Cissus capensis*
Evergreen Pear	*Pyrus kawakami*
False Aralia	*Aralia elegantissima*
False Holly	*Osmanthus ilicifolius*
Fernleaf Acacia	*Acacia baileyana*
Fern-leaf Full-moon Maple	*Acer japonicum 'Aconitifolium'*
Fern Pine	*Podocarpus*
Fig	*Ficus*
Firethorn	*Pyracantha*
Firewheel Tree	*Stenocarpus*
Five Finger Fern	*Adiantum pedatum*
Flannel Bush	*Fremontia californica*
Flame Pea Shrub	*Chorizema varium*
Flaxleaf Paperbark	*Melaleuca linariifolia*
Flowering Crabapple	*Malus*
Flowering Cherry	*Prunus*
Flowering Maple	*Abutilon hybridum*
Flowering Plum	*Prunus*
Flowering Peach	*Prunus*
Flowering Quince	*Cydonia japonica*
Fuchsia Flowering Gooseberry	*Ribies speciosum*
Geraldton Wax Flower	*Chamaelaucium ciliatum*
Germander	*Teucrium fruticans*
Giant Burmese Honeysuckle	*Lonicera hildebrandiana*
Giant Chain Fern	*Woodwardia chamissoi*
Giant Snail Vine	*Phaseolus gigantea*
Glossy Abelia	*Abelia grandiflora*
Glossy Aralia	*Aralia sieboldii*
Gold Dust Plant	*Aucuba japonica 'Variegata'*
Gold Flower	*Hypericum moscrianum*
Golden Bamboo	*Bambusa phyllostachys 'Aurea'*
Golden Chain Tree	*Laburnum vossi*
Golden Rain Tree	*Koelreuteria paniculata*
Grayleafed Cotoneaster	*Cotoneaster glaucophylla*
Grecian Bay	*Laurus nobilis*
Grecian Laurel	*Laurus nobilis*
Guadalupe Fan Palm	*Erythea edulis*
Guinea Gold Vine	*Hibbertia volubilis*
Hopseed Bush	*Dodonaea*
Hemlock	*Tsuga*
Hawthorn	*Crataegus*
Heavenly Bamboo	*Nandina*
Hinoki Cypress	*Chamaecyparis obtusa*
Holly	*Ilex*
Holly Fern	*Cyrtomium falcatum*
Holly Leaf Cherry	*Prunus ilicifolia*
Holly Oak	*Quercus ilex*
Hollywood Juniper	*Jumiper torulosa*
Honey Bush	*Melianthus major*
Honeysuckle	*Lonicera*
Horsechestnut	*Aesculus*
Horsetail Reed Grass	*Equisetum hyemale*
Huckleberry	*Vaccinium*
Incense Cedar	*Libocedrus decurrens*
Indian Laurel	*Ficus retusa nitida*
Indian Long-needled Pine	*Pinus roxburghi*
Irish Yew	*Taxus baccata fastigiata*
Italian Alder	*Alnus cordata*
Italian Buckthorn	*Rhamnus alaternus*
Italian Cypress	*Cupressus sempervirens*
Italian Stone Pine	*Pinus pinea*
Ivy	*Hedera*

Jade Plant	*Crassula argentea*
Japanese Black Pine	*Pinus thunbergi*
Japanese Cedar	*Cryptomeria japonica*
Japanese Coral Bark Maple	*Acer palmatum 'Sangokakis'*
Japanese Green Cutleaf Maple	*Acer palmatum 'Dissectum Virides'*
Japanese Lace Fern	*Polystichum setosum*
Japanese Maple	*Acer palmatum*
Japanese Pittosporum	*Pittosporum tobira*
Japanese Privet	*Ligustrum japonica*
Japanese Red Pine	*Pinus densiflora*
Japanese Spurge	*Pachysandra terminalis*
Jelecote (or Mexican) Pine	*Pinus patula*
Kafir Lily	*Clivia miniata*
Kafir Plum	*Harpephyllum caffrum*
Kangaroo Ivy	*Cissus antarctica*
Kanooka Box	*Tristania laurina*
Karo Pittosporum	*Pittosporum crassifolium*
King Palm	*Seaforthia elegans*
Kinnikinnick	*Arctostaphylos uvaursi*
Kupuka Tree	*Griselinia littoralis*
Laceleaf Japanese Maple	*Acer palmatum 'Dissectum'*
Lady Palm	*Rhapis excelsa*
Lavender	*Lavandula*
Lavender Starflower	*Grewia caffra*
Lavender Trumpet Vine	*Bignonia violacea*
Leather Leaf Fern	*Aspidium capense*
Lemonleaf	*Gaultheria*
Lemon Verbena	*Lippia citriodora*
Lemonade Berry	*Rhus integrifolia*
Lemon Scented Gum	*Eucalyptus citriodora*
Lilac	*Syringa vulgaris*
Lilac Melaleuca	*Melaleuca decussata*
Lily of the Nile	*Agapanthus africanus*
Lily of the Valley Shrub	*Pieris japonica*
Lily Turfs	*Liriope muscari*
Linden	*Tilia*
Locust	*Robinia (also Gleditsia)*
Lombardy Popular	*Populus nigra italica*
Loquat	*Eriobotrya*
Madagascar Jasmine	*Stephanotis floribunda*
Madrone	*Arbutus menziesii*
Maidenhair Tree	*Ginkgo*
Manzanita	*Arctostaphylos*
Matilija Poppy	*Romneya coulteri*
Mayten Tree	*Maytenus*
Mediterranean Fan Palm	*Chamaerops humilis*
Mexican Blue Palm	*Erythea armata*
Mexican Fan Palm	*Washingtonia robusta*
Mexican Orange	*Choisya ternata*
Mexican (or Jelecote) Pine	*Pinus patula*
Meyer Lemon	*Citrus*
Mimosa	*Albizia julibrissin*
Mirror Plant	*Coprosma*
Mock Orange	*Philadelphus virginalis*
Modesto Ash	*Fraxinus velutina 'Glabra'*
Monkey Tree	*Auracaria auracana*
Monterey Cypress	*Cupressus macrocarpa*
Monterey Manzanita	*Arctostaphylos hookeri*
Monterey Pine	*Pinus radiata*
Moraine Locust	*Gleditsia*
Morrocco Creeper	*Convolvulus mauritanicus*
Mother Fern	*Asplenium bulbiferum*
Mountain Ash	*Sorbus*

Mountain Laurel	*Kalmia latifolia*
Mugho Pine	*Pinus mugo mughus*
Mulberry	*Morus*
Myrtle	*Myrtus*
Natal Plum	*Carissa*
Neantha Bella Palm	*Chamaedorea elegans*
Nest Spruce	*Picea excelsa nidiformis*
New Zealand Christmas Tree	*Metrosideros*
New Zealand Flax	*Phormium tenax*
Night Blooming Jasmine	*Cestrum parqui*
Norfolk Island Pine	*Araucaria excelsa*
Norway Maple	*Acer platanoides*
Norway Spruce	*Picea excelsa, (P. abies)*
Oleander	*Nerium*
Olive	*Olea*
Orange Jessamine	*Murraya exotica*
Orchid Tree	*Bauhinia purpurea*
Oregon Grape	*Mahonia aquifolium*
Pacific or Western Dogwood	*Cornus nuttallii*
Paper Birch	*Betula papyrifera*
Parrot Bill	*Clianthus puniceus*
Passion Fruit	*Passiflora edulis*
Passion Vine	*Passiflora pfordtii*
Persian Lilac	*Syringa persica*
Persimmon	*Diospyros*
Pin Oak	*Quercus palustris*
Pineapple Guava	*Feijoa*
Pink Acacia	*Albizia julibrissin*
Pink Abelia	*Abelia 'Edward Goucher'*
Pink Breath of Heaven	*Diosma pulchrum*
Pink Jasmine	*Jasminum polyanthum*
Pink Powder Puff	*Calliandra inequilatera*
Pistachio	*Pistacia chinensis*
Plume Cryptomeria	*Cryptomeria japonica elegans*
Pomegranate	*Punica granatum*
Pony Tail	*Beaucarnea recurvata*
Portugal Laurel	*Prunus lusitanica*
Potato Vine	*Solanum jasminoides*
Port Orford Cedar	*Chamaecyparis lawsoniana*
Pride of Madeira	*Echium fastuosum*
Primrose Jasmine	*Jasminum primulinum*
Princess Flower	*Pleroma grandiflora*
Privet	*Ligustrum*
Purple Leaf Acacia	*Acacia baileyana 'Purpurea'*
Pygmy Date Palm	*Phoenix roebelenii*
Queensland Nut	*Macadamia*
Queen Palm	*Cocos plumosa*
Rangpur Lime	*Citrus*
Red Bay	*Persea borbonia*
Redbud	*Cercis*
Red Clusterberry Cotoneaster	*Cotoneaster parneyi*
Red Cutleaf Maple	*Acer palmatum 'Alissectum'*
Red Flowering Currant	*Ribes sanguineum*
Red Flowering Eucalyptus	*Eucalyptus ficifolia*
Red Gum	*Eucalyptus rostrata*
Red Horse Chestnut	*Aesculus carnea 'Briotii'*
Red Iron Bark	*Eucalyptus sideroxylon rosea*
Red Japanese Maple	*Acer palmatum 'Atropurpurium'*
Red Leaf Banana	*Musa maurelii*
Red Strawberry Guava	*Psidium cattleianum*
Ribbon Gum	*Eucalyptus viminalis*
Rice Paper Plant	*Aralia papyrifera*
Rock Cotoneaster	*Cotoneaster horizontalis*

Rock Daphne	*Daphne cneorum*
Rock Rose	*Cistus*
Rockspray Cotoneaster	*Cotoneaster microphylla*
Rose Bottle Bush	*Melaleuca nesophila*
Rosemary	*Rosmarinus*
Rose of Sharon	*Althaea syriaca*
Round Leaf Fern	*Pellaea rotundifolia*
Roundleaf Laurestinus	*Viburnum tinus robustum*
Roundleaf Indian Hawthorn	*Raphiolepis ovata*
Rubber Tree	*Ficus elastica decora*
Sago Palm	*Cycas revoluta*
Salal	*Gaultheria*
Sandankwa	*Viburnum suspensum*
Scarlet Oak	*Quercus coccinea*
Scarlet Trumpet Vine	*Bignonia cherere*
Scarlet Wisteria Tree	*Daubentonia tripetii*
Schwedler Purple Leaf Maple	*Acer plataniodes* 'Schwedleri'
Scotch Broom	*Cytisus*
Scotch Heather	*Calluna vulgaris*
Scotch Pine	*Pinus sylvestris*
Sea Urchin Tree	*Hakea laurina*
Senegal Date Palm	*Phoenix reclinata*
Senisa	*Leucophyllum frutescens*
Shademaster Locust	*Gleditsia*
Shamel Ash	*Fraxinus uhdei*
Shore Juniper	*Juniper conferta*
Shoe Button Spiraea	*Spiraea prunifolia*
Shrimp Plant	*Beloperone guttata*
Shrubby Yew	*Podocarpus maki*
Siberian Grape	*Mahonia bealei*
Silver Lace Vine	*Polygonum aubertii*
Silk Tassel Bush	*Garrya elliptica*
Silk Oak Tree	*Grevillea robusta*
Silver Berry	*Elaeagnus*
Silver Dollar Eucalyptus	*Eucalyptus polyanthemos*
Silver Leaf Cotoneaster	*Cotoneaster pannosa*
Silver Maple	*Acer saccharinum*
Silver Mountain Gum	*Eucalyptus pulverulenta*
Silver Tree	*Leucadendron*
Single Mother Fern	*Polystichum angulare*
Smoke Tree	*Cotinus coggygria, Rhus cotinus*
Snail Seed	*Cocculus*
Snowball	*Viburnum opulus sterile*
Sourwood Sorrel Tree	*Oxydendrum arboreum*
Southern Magnolia	*Magnolia grandiflora*
Spanish Bayonet	*Yucca aloifolia*
Spanish Broom	*Spartium junceum*
Spanish Dagger	*Yucca gloriosa*
Staghorn Fern	*Platycerium*
Star Acacia	*Acacia verticillata*
Star Jasmine	*Rhynchospermum jasminoides*
Star Pine	*Araucaria excelsa*
St. John's Bread	*Ceratonia siliqua*
St. Johnswort	*Hypericum patulum henryi*
Strawberry Tree	*Arbutus unedo*
Sugar Bush	*Rhus ovata*
Sugar Plum Tree	*Lagunaria pattersoni*
Sumac	*Rhus typhina*
Sunburst Locust	*Gleditsia*
Swamp Tea Tree	*Melaleuca leucadendra*
Sweet Broom	*Genista racemosa*
Sweetgum	*Liquidambar*
Sweet Olive	*Osmanthus fragrans*

Sweet Pea Shrub	*Polygala dalmaisiana*
Sweetshade	*Hymenosporum flavum*
Sweetspire	*Itea*
Sweet Viburnum	*Viburnum odoratissimum*
Sycamore	*Platanus*
Sydney Golden Wattle	*Acacia longifolia*
Table Mountain Pine	*Pinus densiflora 'Umbraculifera'*
Tamarisk	*Tamarix tetrandra*
Tanyosho Pine	*Pinus densiflora 'Umbraculifera'*
Tarata Pittosporum	*Pittosporum eugenioides*
Tasmanian Tree Fern	*Dicksonia antarctica*
Tawhiwhi Pittosporum	*Pittosporum tenuifolium (P. nigricans)*
Tea Tree	*Leptospermum*
Tecomaria	*Tecoma*
Texas Sage	*Leucophyllum frutescens*
Texas Umbrella Tree	*Melia*
Threadbranch Cypress	*Chamaecyparis filifera*
Toyon	*Photinia arbutifolia*
Trumpet Vine	*Bignonia*
Trumpet Creeper	*Campsis tagliabuana*
Tulip Tree	*Deciduous magnolia*
Tulip Tree	*Liriodendron*
Umbrella Pine	*Sciadopitys verticillata*
Umbrella Tree	*Tupidanthus calyptratus*
Victorian Box	*Pittosporum undulatum*
Victorian Rosemary	*Westringia rosmariniformis*
Vine Maple	*Acer circinatum*
Virginia Creeper	*Ampelopsis quinquefolia*
Weeping Fig	*Ficus benjamina*
Western Sword Fern	*Polystichum munitum*
White Alder	*Alnus rhombifolia*
White Birch	*Betula alba*
White Fir	*Abies concolor*
White Horse Chestnut	*Aesculus hipposcastamum*
White Iron Bark	*Eucalyptus leucoxylon*
Wild Lilac	*Ceanothus*
Willow	*Salix*
Windmill Palm	*Chamaerops excelsa*
Yellow Trumpet Vine	*Bignonia chamberlaynii*
Yesterday Today and Tomorrow	*Brunfelsia*
Yew	*Taxus*
Yew Pine	*Podocarpus macrophyllus*
Yucca Pendula	*Yucca recurvifolia*
Zabel Laurel	*Prunus laurocerasus 'Zabeliana'*

PLANTS WITH WHITE FLOWERS

Abelia	Escallonia	Nerium
Azalea	Eugenia	Osmanthus
Acanthus	Gardenia	Philadelphus
Aesculus	Gleditsia	Photinia
Althaea	Hebe	Pieris
Bouvardia	Hibiscus	Pittosporum
Calluna	Hydrangea	Polygonum
Camellia	Jasminum	Prunus
Carissa	Lantana	Pyracantha
Carpenteria	Leptospermum	Raphiolepis
Catalpa	Leucothoe	Rhododendron
Choisya	Ligustrum	Rhynchospermum
Cistus	Loropetalum	Romneya
Clematis	Lyonothamnus	Solanum
Convolvulus	Magnolia	Sparmannis
Cornus	Malus	Spiraea
Cortaderia	Marguerite	Stephanotis
Crataegus	Melaleuca	Syringa
Cytissus	Moraea	Viburnum
Datura	Murraya	Wisteria
Deutzia	Myrtus	Yucca
Diosma	Nandina	

PLANTS WITH YELLOW TO ORANGE FLOWERS

Abutilon	Euryops	Koelreuteria
Acacia	Fremontia	Lonicera
Azalea	Gelsemium	Mahonia
Berberis	Genista	Marguerite
Bignonia	Grevillea	Poinciana
Bougainvillea	Hibbertia	Rhododendron
Cassia	Hibiscus	Solandra
Clivia	Hymenosporum	Spartium
Corokia	Hypericum	Strelitzia
Crotalaria	Jasmine	Streptosolen
Cytisus	Kerria	Thunbergia
Daubentonia		

PLANTS WITH RED OR PINK FLOWERS

Abelia
Abutilon
Albizia
Aesculus
Azalea
Bignonia
Bougainvillea
Calliandra
Callistemon
Calluna
Camellia
Campsis
Ceris
Chorisia
Clematis
Cornus
Crataegus

Correa
Cyponia
Daphne
Diosma
Erica
Escallonia
Eucalyptus
Fuchsia
Hibiscus
Hydrangea
Kalmia
Kolkwitzia
Lagerstroemia
Lagunaria
Lantana
Leptospernum
Magnolia

Malus
Mandevilla
Melianthus
Melaleuca
Metrosideros
Nerium
Passiflora
Prunus
Punica
Raphiolepis
Rhododendron
Ribes
Stenocarpus
Tamarix
Tecoma
Weigela
Wisteria

PLANTS WITH BLUE OR VIOLET FLOWERS

Azalea
Bauhinia
Bignonia
Bougainvillea
Brunsfelsia
Ceanothus
Ceratostigma
Clematis
Echium
Fuchsia

Grewia
Hardenbergia
Hebe
Jacaranda
Lantana
Lavandula
Leucophyllum
Liriope
Melia
Paulownia

Pleroma
Plumbago
Polygala
Rosmarinus
Solanum
Sollya
Syringa
Teucrium
Veronica
Wisteria

FRAGRANT TREES AND SHRUBS

Acacia	*Eucalyptus*	*Myrtus*
Baccharis	*Gardenia*	*Osmanthus*
Bouvardia	*Hymenosporum*	*Philadelphus*
Brunfelsia	*Jasmine*	*Pittosporum*
Camphor	*Laurus*	*Rhododendrons*
Carissa	*Lavandula*	*Robinia*
Cestrum	*Ligustrum*	*Rhynchospermum*
Choisya	*Libocedrus*	*Rosmarinus*
Citrus	*Lippia*	*Sarcococca*
Clematis	*Lonicera*	*Spartium*
Cypress	*Magnolia*	*Stephanotis*
Daphne	*Mandevilla*	*Syringa*
Datura	*Michelia*	*Viburnum*
Diosma	*Murraya*	*Wisteria*

SEASHORE PLANTS

Abelia	*Euryops*	*Metrosideros*
Acacia	*Fraxinus*	*Myoporum*
Barberry	*Garrya*	*Myrica*
Camphor	*Gaultheria*	*Pittosporum*
Ceratonia	*Gelsemium*	*Plumbago*
Ceratostigma	*Griselinia*	*Raphiolepis*
Cistus	*Hakea*	*Rhus ovata*
Coprosma	*Hebe*	*Rosmarinus*
Correa	*Hypericum*	*Schinus*
Corynocarpus	*Juniper*	*Solandra*
Cupaniopsis	*Lantana*	*Spartium*
Cupressus	*Leptospermum*	*Tecoma*
Dracaena	*Leucophyllum*	*Ulmus*
Duranta	*Liquidambar*	*Viburnum*
Echium	*Lonicera*	*Veronica*
Escallonia	*Marguerites*	
Eugenia	*Melaleuca*	

TREES AND SHRUBS FOR DRY PLACES

Abelia
Acacia
Albizia
Arbutus
Arctostaphylos
Atriplex
Baccharis
Berberis
Buddleia
Buxus
Callistemon
Cassia
Ceanothus
Ceratonia
Cercis
Chamaelaucium
Cistus
Cordyline
Cortaderia
Cotoneaster

Cotinus
Cupressus
Cytisus
Dodonaea
Echium
Eleagnus
Eriogonum
Eucalyptus
Feijoa
Fremontia
Garrya
Grevillea
Hakea
Hypericum
Juniper
Lagerstroemia
Lantana
Lavandula
Leptospermum
Mahonia

Melaleuca
Myoporum
Nerium
Olea
Pinus
Phormium
Pittosporum
Prunus
Pyracantha
Quercus
Rhamnus
Rhus
Robinia
Rosmarinus
Schinus
Senecio
Sorbus
Xylosma
Yucca

TREES AND SHRUBS FOR DAMP PLACES

Abutilon
Acer
Alnus
Aucuba
Bamboo
Betula
Clivia
Coprosma

Cornus
Cyperus
Equisetum
Fraxinus
Fuchsia
Kalmia
Leucothoe
Ligustrum

Lonicera
Metasequoia
Salix
Sequoia
Skimmia
Solandra
Spiraea

DEER-RESISTANT PLANTS FOR ORNAMENTAL USE*

Abies spp
Abutilon spp
Acacia spp
Acer negundo
Acer palmatum
Agapanthus africanus
Agave spp
Ajuga spp
Albizia spp
Aloe spp
Araucaria spp
Arbutus unedo
Beaucarnea recurvata
Berberis spp
Brachychiton populneum
Buddleia davidii
Buxus spp
Cactaceae spp
Calliandra tweedii
Calycanthus occidentalis
Carpenteria californica
Cassia spp
Casuarina stricta
Cedrus spp
Ceratonia siliqua
Cercis occidentalis
Chamaecyparis spp
Chamaerops humilis
Choisya ternata
Chrysanthemum frutescens
Chrysanthemum maximum
Cistus spp
Clematis spp
Coprosma repens
Cordyline australis
Cornus capitata
Correa spp
Cotinus coggygria
Cotoneaster spp
Crataegus spp
Cupressus spp

Cycas spp
Cytisus scoparius
Daphne spp
Datura spp
Delphinium spp
Diosma ericoides
Diosma pulchrum
Diospyros
Dodonaea viscosa
Echium fastuosum
Erythea armata
Erythea edulis
Escallonia spp
Eucalyptus spp
Ficus spp
Forsythia
Fraxinus velutina
Fraxinus velutina glabra
Gaultheria shallon
Gelsemium sempervirens
Genista monosperma
Ginkgo biloba
Hakea suaveolens
Hedera
Helleborus spp
Ilex spp
Iris spp
Jasminum spp
Juniperus spp
Kerria japonica
Kniphofia uvaria
Lantana
Lavandula spp
Leptospermum spp
Lyonothamnus floribundus
Magnolia spp
Mahonia spp
Maytenus boaria
Melaleuca leucadendra
Melianthus major
Mesembryanthemum spp

Metrosideros tomentosa
Myoporum laetum
Myrica californica
Myrtus communis
Nandina domestica
Nerium oleander
Olea europaea
Osteospermum fruiticosum
Paeonia suffruticosa
Parkinsonia aculeata
Penstemon spp
Phoenix spp
Phormium tenax
Picea spp
Pinus spp
Pittosporum spp
Plantanus racemosa
Potentilla fruticosa
Prunus caroliniana
Rhododendron spp.
  (except Azalea-leaved varieties)
Rhus ovata
Robinia pseudoacacia
Romneya coulteri
Rosmarinus officinalis
Sambucus
Scabiosa spp
Schinus
Solanum spp
Spartium junceum
Syringa vulgaris
Syzygium puniculatum
Taxus spp
Tecomaria capensis
Teucrium fruticans
Thuja spp
Trachycarpus fortunei
Tradescantia spp
Vinca spp
Washingtonia spp
Yucca spp

*Some of the plants will be resistant in some areas and not in others.

PLANTS RESISTANT
TO ARMILLARIA ROOT ROT (OAK ROOT FUNGUS)

ORNAMENTALS
IMMUNE OR HIGHLY RESISTANT

Botanic Name	Common Name	Botanic Name	Common Name
Abies concolor	Colorado or White Fir	*Brachychiton populneum*	Kurrajong Bottle Tree
Acacia decurrens var. mollis	Black Wattle	*Buxus sempervirens*	Common Box
Acacia latifolia	Acacia	*Ilex aquifolium*	English Holly
Acacia verticillata	Star Acacia	*Lonicera nitida*	Bush or Box Honeysuckle
Acer macrophyllum	Big-Leaf Maple	*Pinus canariensis*	Canary Pine
Arbutus menziesii	Madrone	*Pinus Torreyana*	Torrey Pine
Berberis aquifolium	Oregon Grape	*Prunus ilicifoli* Holly-leaved Cherry	
Berberis nevinii	Nevin Mahonia	*Prunus lyonii* Catalina Cherry	

MODERATELY RESISTANT

Botanic Name	Common Name	Botanic Name	Common Name
Abelia grandiflora	Glossy Abelia	*Ligustrum japonicum*	Japanese Privet
Acer negundo var. californicum	California Box Elder	*Malus prunifolia*	Pear-leaf Crab Apple
Berberis darwinii	Darwin Barberry	*Myrtus communis*	True Myrtle
Berberis thunbergii	Japanese Barbery	*Pittosporum tobira*	Japanese Pittosporum
Berberis wilsoniae	Wilson Barberry	*Prunus sp*	Black Damas Plum
Chamaecyparis lawsoniana	Lawson Cypress	*Prunus avium*	Mazzard Sweet Cherry
Cydonia oblonga	Quince	*Prunus Salicina*	Satsuma Plum
Elaeagnus commutata	Silverberry	*Prunus Mexicana*	Big Tree Plum
Euonymus japonica	Evergreen Burning Bush	*Prunus Mume*	Japanese Apricot
Grevillea robusta	Silk Oak	*Pseudotsuga menziesli*	Douglas Fir
Hebe andersonii	Anderson Speedwell	*Pyracantha coccinea*	Scarlet Firethorn
Hebe speciosa	Showy or Imperial Speedwell	*Pyracantha lalandii*	Laland Firethorn
		Spiraea prunifolia	Bridal Wreath Spirea

RESISTANT

Botanic Name	Common Name	Botanic Name	Common Name
Abutilon spp	Abutilon or Flowering Maple	*Liriodendron tulipifera*	Tulip Tree
Arctostaphylos spp	Manzanita	*Morus spp*	Mulberry
Catalpa spp	Catalpa	*Nerium oleander*	Oleander
Ceanothus spp	Ceanothus	*Philadelphus spp*	Mock-Orange
Cinnamon camphora	Camphor Tree	*Pittosporum spp*	Pittosporum
Cistus spp	Rock Rose	*Platanus spp*	Plane Tree or Sycamore
Eugenia spp	Eugenia	*Rhaphiolepis spp*	Rhaphiolepis
Eucalyptus spp	Eucalyptus	*Rhus spp*	Sumac
Fraxinus spp	Ash	*Robinia spp*	Locust
Hebe spp	Hebe	*Tamarix aphylla*	Tamarisk, Athel
Hedera helix	Ivy	*Tibouchina semidecandra*	
Hibiscus spp	Rose Mallow and Hibiscus		Pleroma, Glorybush or Princess Flower
Lagerstroemia indica	Crape-Myrtle	*Ulmus spp*	Elm
Liquidambar stryaciflua	Sweet Gum	Various genera	Palms

IMMUNE OR HIGHLY RESISTANT

Botanic Name	Common Name	Botanic Name	Common Name
Carya illinoensis	Pecan	*Juglans hindsii*	California Black Walnut
Castanea dentata	American Chestnut	*Malus loensis*	Prairie Crab Apple
Castanea sativa	European Chestnut	*Malus sp*	French Crab Apple
Diospyros kaki	Japanese Persimmon	*Persea americana*	Mexican Avocado
Diospyros virginiana	Common Persimmon	*Prunus americana*	American Plum
Ficus carica cv. kadota	Kadota Fig	*Prunus cerasifera*	Myrobalan Plum
Ficus carica cv. mission	Mission Fig	*Pyrus communis*	French Pear

AFTERWORD

In the Introduction of this book I told you of the aims I had in mind when I wrote it.

Now, in Conclusion—let me add that it is time to stop talking to your plants all the time and *listen* (with your eyes) for a change. They will tell you of their aches and pains—yellow, droopy, brown-edged leaves and/or bent-over, stringy branches and plants reaching for the light—and, in many other ways.

I hope you enjoy this work.

Gordon Courtright